ON DIVINATION
AND SYNCHRONICITY

Marie-Louise von Franz, Honorary Patron

STUDIES IN JUNGIAN PSYCHOLOGY
BY JUNGIAN ANALYSTS

Daryl Sharp, General Editor

ON DIVINATION
AND SYNCHRONICITY

The Psychology of Meaningful Chance

MARIE-LOUISE VON FRANZ

Canadian Cataloguing in Publication Data

Franz, Marie-Louise von, 1915-
  On divination and synchronicity

(Studies in Jungian psychology ; 3)
Based on a series of lectures delivered in 1969 at
the C.G. Jung Institute in Zurich, Switzerland.
Includes index.

ISBN 0-919123-02-3

1. Coincidence in psychical research — Psychological
aspects. 2. Divination. 3. Psychical research. 4. Jung,
Carl Gustav, 1875-1961.
I. Title. II. Series.

BF1175.F72   133   C80-094576-X

INNER CITY BOOKS
Box 1271, Station Q, Toronto, Canada M4T 2P4

Honorary Patron: Marie-Louise von Franz
Publisher and General Editor: Daryl Sharp
Editorial Board: Fraser Boa, Daryl Sharp, Marion Woodman

INNER CITY BOOKS is devoted to the publication of Studies in
Jungian Psychology by Jungian Analysts. Inquiries regarding
manuscripts may be addressed to the Editor.

*Marie-Louise von Franz is a Jungian Analyst practising in Küsnacht,
Switzerland.*

Cover Photo by Dave Sharp. Illustrations by Ann Yeoman.

Set in Baskerville by Blain Berdan, Toronto.
Printed and bound in Canada by Webcom Limited.

CONTENTS

Please see final pages for  *Catalogue and Order Form*

This book is based on the transcription by Miss Una Thomas of the lecture series presented by Dr. von Franz at the C.G. Jung Institute, Zürich, in the fall of 1969. The author and publisher are grateful to Miss Thomas for her faithful preparation of the original version. The text in its present form was edited for publication by Daryl Sharp and Marion Woodman. The index was compiled by Daryl Sharp.

Lecture 1

You may perhaps know of the amusing fact that originally divination was always practised in churches. The old Jews, for instance, had a divination oracle in their sanctuaries in Jerusalem and on certain occasions when the priest wanted to consult Jahweh he tried through such oracles to discover the will of God. In all primitive civilizations divination techniques have been used to find out what God, or the gods, want, but in time this has been discontinued and outgrown; it has become a dark, magical, and despised practice, but today this lecture is being given in the *Kirchgemeinde* (parish church), a nice little synchronicity.

The view of the world which Jung tried to bring back into focus, and on which divination basically rests, is that of synchronicity; therefore before we go into details about the problems of divination we have to remember what Jung said about synchronicity. In his Foreword to the English edition of Richard Wilhelm's translation of *The I Ching or Book of Changes*, he gives a very good summary of the difference between causal and synchronistic thinking. Causal thinking is, so to speak, lineal. There is a sequence of events A, B, C, D, and you think backwards and wonder why D appears because of C, why C appears because of B, and why B because of A, like some kind of inner or outer event. One tries to trace back in one's mind why these coordinate effects have worked.

We know that through the investigations of modern physicists it has now been proved that on the microphysical level this principle is no longer completely valid; we can no longer think of causality as absolute law, but only as a tendency or prevailing probability. So causality is shown to be a way of thinking which satisfies our mental grasp of a cluster of physical events, but does not complete-

7

ly get at the core of natural laws, it only delineates general trends or possibilities. Synchronistic thinking, on the other hand, one could call field thinking, the centre of which is time.

Time also comes into causality since we normally think that the cause comes before the effect. In modern physics it sometimes looks as if the effect came before the cause, and therefore they try to turn it round and say that you could still call that causal; but I think Jung is right in saying that that is enlarging and twisting the idea of causality *ad absurdum* so far that it loses its meaning. Normally, cause always comes before effect, so there also is a lineal idea of time, before and after, with the effect always after the before.

Synchronistic thinking, the classic way of thinking in China, is thinking in fields, so to speak. In Chinese philosophy such thinking has been developed and differentiated much more than in any other civilization; there the question is not why has this come about, or what factor caused this effect, but what likes to happen together in a meaningful way in the same moment? The Chinese always ask: "What tends to happen together in time?" So the centre of their field concept would be a time moment on which are clustered the events A,B,C,D, and so on (Figure 1).

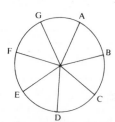

Figure 1. Field of time
(time-bound ensemble of events).

Richard Wilhelm puts it very well in his Introduction to the *I Ching* where he speaks of the complex of events which occur at a certain time moment.

In our causal thinking we have made a big separation between psychic events and physical events, and we only watch to see how physical events produce, or have a causal effect upon, each other and on psychological events. Right up to the 19th century the idea still persisted in the sciences (and it still does in those less de-

8

veloped) that only physical causes have physical effects and psychic causes psychological effects; for instance, Freud's way of thinking: "This woman is neurotic and has an idiosyncrasy as the result of a childhood trauma." That would be the same kind of thinking but transposed onto the psychological level.

The question now being asked is whether there are interactions between those two lines. Is there something like a psychic cause for physical events and vice versa? That is a problem of psychosomatic medicine. Interactions between those two chains of causality can be proved: you may read a letter saying that somebody you loved very much has died, and get physiological effects; you may even faint, a reaction caused not by the ink and the paper, but by the psychic content of the communication. There is a causal interaction between those two lines which one is only now beginning to investigate.

The synchronistic, i.e., the Chinese way of thinking, however, is completely different. It is a differentiation of primitive thinking in which no difference has ever been made between psychological and physical facts. In their question as to what likes to occur together, one can bring in both inner and outer facts. For the synchronistic way of thinking it is even essential to watch both areas of reality, the physical and the psychic, and to notice that at the moment when one had these and these thoughts or these and these dreams — which would be psychological events — such and such outer physical events happened; i.e., there was a complex of physical and psychological events. Though causal thinking also poses the problem of time in some form because of the before and after, the problem of time is much more central in the synchronistic way of thinking because there it is the key moment — a certain moment in time — which is the uniting fact, the focal point for the observation of this complex of events.

In modern Western science, algebraic means are used to describe the probabilities of the sequence of events — algebraic matrices of different forms and algebraic functions and curves. The Chinese also use mathematics for the description of *their* laws of synchronicity. They use something like mathematical matrices but not algebraic abstractions; they use the individual natural integers (1, 2, 3, 4, 5, 6, 7), so one could say that the mathematics of *this* Chinese way of thinking would be the different qualifications one can draw from the series of natural integers, the common laws which

9

one can abstract from them. One uses the 3, 4, and 5 to grasp a cluster of events in a mathematical form.

The basis of the science of mathematics, or the scientific mathematics of synchronistic thinking, is therefore the series of natural integers, and one finds that in all techniques of divination. The simplest form of divination is the binary: hit or miss. One throws a coin and gets heads or tails and accordingly decides whether one will go or not to the Rigi, or whichever direction you are undetermined about. Hit or miss is the basic idea of all divination but in different civilizations there are differentiated techniques by which to read the situation better at a certain time moment.

The Western way of thinking is an extraverted orientation, namely first to look at the events and then to abstract a mathematical model. The Eastern, or Chinese way, is to use an intuitive mental model to read the event, namely natural integers. They turn first to the event of throwing heads or tails, that is a psychic and a psycho-physical event. The question of the diviner is psychic, while the event is that the coin falls either heads or tails, from which the further outer and inner events can be read. So it is an outlook completely complementary to ours.

What is important in China, as Jung also pointed out in his essay called "Synchronicity: An Acausal Connecting Principle," is that the Chinese did not get stuck, like many other primitive civilizations do, into using divination methods only to predict the future — whether for instance one should marry or not. One asks the priest and he says: "No, you won't" — or you will — "get her." That is something practised all over the world, not only officially but by many people quite silently in their rooms when they lay Tarot cards, etc., or they have little rituals: "If today the sun shines, then I'll do such and such a thing." Man constantly thinks that way and even scientists have these little superstitions, telling themselves that because the sun shone into their room when they got up they knew that today this and this would come off right. Even if one discards it in one's conscious *Weltanschauung*, the primitive man in us constantly uses this kind of prognostication of the future with the left hand, so to speak, and then shamefacedly denies it to his rationalistic brother, though he is much relieved to discover that the other does that too!

In this stage divination cannot evolve and become differentiated; it remains a kind of primitive guessing technique, trying to guess

Wanting a short cut!

the future by some technical means. That is practised, as I say, by us and more openly in all primitive civilizations. If one wants to travel in Africa one goes to a medicine man who throws a few chicken bones, and according to the way they fall, whether more into the red or the white section he has drawn on the ground, and in what constellation, he will say whether the journey will be successful or not, and whether to go or not. Before any big enterprise, such as hunting or making a long dangerous journey to Johannesburg, or whatever it is, one first always consults such an oracle and then acts accordingly. We do the same thing more secretly but in both cases — I'll mention some exceptions later — it is not built into the *Weltanschauung* and therefore remains a kind of undeveloped primitive practice, a ritual game, so to speak, which we tend not to integrate into our conscious view of reality.

The Chinese, like all primitive civilizations, still had this primitive technique until it was forbidden. In the market place of every Chinese town there were a few I Ching priests who would throw coins for you or take the yarrow stalks, and get answers to your questions, but then it was forbidden. In 1960 Mao thought of slightly releasing the rationalistic political pressure on the masses and found out that there were two possibilities: either to give more rice, or to allow the use of the I Ching, and all those whom he consulted told him that the people were more eager to use the I Ching again than to get more food. Spiritual food, and the I Ching was their spiritual food, was more important to them, so it was allowed for I think one or two years and then he strangled it again. It is very typical for the Chinese that even a bowl of rice — and they are very hungry — was less important than again to have their beloved Book of Changes and its spiritual orientation.

The great merit of the I Ching is due to two remarkable geniuses, namely the legendary King Wên and the Duke of Chou, who developed what was originally a primitive oracle system into a complete philosophic *Weltanschauung*. They treated the oracle and its ethical consequences philosophically; they thought about its psychological consequences and presuppositions and through that it has in China become the basis of a very deep and very broad *Weltanschauung*. Jung writes in his paper on synchronicity that this has happened only in China, but I chanced to discover that it has also happened in Western Nigeria. There were certain medicine men there who by their oracle technique — geomancy in their case —

11

world view.

developed a whole religious philosophy, naturally slightly more primitive than the Chinese one, but also a complete religious and philosophical viewpoint about the oracle, not using it just as a prognostication technique.

Those are the two instances of which I know. There is probably a third, but I have not been able to get hold of the material; as far as I can find out only one paper has been written on it, but I cannot get hold of it anywhere. The old Mayan civilization which, as has become more and more evident, is dependent on central Asia and therefore linked up with the Chinese civilization, also had an I Ching type of oracle technique, and I would guess from the quality of their civilization that they also had a philosophical outlook and viewpoint about it and that it was not just a left hand prognostication technique. One man, Schultze-Jena, published a small paper on it, but though I have been chasing that for two years I cannot find it anywhere in Switzerland, and as far as I know the author only writes of the techniques of the Mayan oracle and not of its philosophical background. We can, however, do some guessing about this because in Mayan philosophy all the gods were time and number gods. All the main figures of the Mayan myths have a specific number which is even expressed in their names. The greatest hero, for instance, is Hunabku — the name comes from Hun, meaning one — and then there is the great hero Seven Hunter; every great god is both a number and a time moment in the calender year. So there is a union of an archetypal figure with a certain time moment and a certain natural integer. This gives a hint that probably the Mayan oracle was philosophically linked with that kind of view, but as I say I have not yet found any details on it.

Let us therefore stay for the moment with the Chinese way of thinking. There is an excellent book on this by the sociologist Marcel Granet, *La Pensée Chinoise,* who says that the Chinese never thought in quantities but always in terms of qualitative emblems. Jung would have said "symbols," and I will use that term so as to make it simpler for us. According to the Chinese, numbers describe regular relationships of events and things, exactly as they do for us. We try with mathematical algebraic formulae to describe regular relationships. As a category, causality is the idea for discovering such relationships, and for the Chinese too, numbers express the regular relationship of things — not in their quantitative way, but in their qualitative hierarchy they qualify the concrete orderedness of things. We could not disagree with that for it is more or less the same as with us, except that their accent is on the quality level.

But it goes further in China, where they believe that the universe probably has an ultimate basic numerical rhythm. The same question arises with us now, for in modern physics it is thought that one might possibly find one basic rhythm of the universe which would explain all the different phenomena, but for us that is at present just a kind of speculative idea held by some modern physicists. The Chinese simply assumed that this rhythm of all reality existed, that it was a number pattern, and that all relationships of things with each other in all areas of outer and inner life therefore mirror this same basic number pattern in a form conceived as a rhythm.

Until the end of the 19th century, the Chinese also had a much more energetic and dynamic outlook on the world than we had, believing that everything was energy in flux. Actually we now think the same but we arrived at the idea much later and by scientific means. Their primary assumption from all time was that everything is outwardly and inwardly a flux of energy, which follows certain basic and recurring numerical rhythms. In all areas of events one would always finally arrive at this mirror image, the basic rhythm — a matrix — of the cosmos. For those who are not so mathematically minded, a matrix is any regular array of numbers in several columns; there may be any number of rows and columns, but always in a rectangular arrangement.

4	9	2
3	5	7
8	1	6

Figure 2. *Lo Shou.* In modern parlance, a matrix.

7
2
8 3 5 4 9
1
6

Figure 3. *Ho-tou.*

For the Chinese one of the basic matrices, or arrangements of the universe, was a quadrangular matrix — a magic square called the *Lo Shou* (Figure 2), which sets the basic rhythm. It is a so-called magic square because whichever way you add up the figures the result is always 15, and it is also the only magic square which has only three

13

elements in each row or column. So it is really a mathematically unique thing. There are many magic squares with more rows and more possibilities of addition, but the simplest is this one and it has only eight solutions. I would say it is one of the most highly symmetrical number matrices to be found in arithmetic. The Chinese discovered it intuitively and for them it represented a basic mirror or rhythmic image of the universe seen in its time aspect. I will return to that later.

The Chinese had two ideas or aspects of time: namely *timeless time* or eternity, unchanging eternity, with superimposed on it *cyclic time*. We live normally, with our consciousness, in cyclic time, according to Chinese ideas, but there is an eternal time — *une durée créatrice*, to use an expression of Bergson's — underneath, which sometimes interferes with the other. Ordinary Chinese time is cyclical and follows this pattern. They arranged the innermost chambers of their imperial palace on such a pattern; also all musical instruments were tuned according to it, all dances and all protocol, as well as what a Mandarin and what a commoner had to do at the funeral of his father. In every detail this number pattern always played a role, because it was thought to be the basic rhythm of reality; therefore in different variations in music, in protocol, in architecture, everywhere this same pattern was always put in the centre.

The underlying numerical order of eternity is called the *Ho-tou* (Figure 3), a mandala and also a cross. There is again 5 in the middle. One counts 1, 2, 3, 4, and then moves to the middle 5, then 6, 7, 8, 9, and then back to 10 — 10 would really be in the middle. One must always cross and come back to the middle. Actually it is the movement of a musical dance because it always emanates into four and contracts into the middle — it has a systole and diastole movement. The *Lo Shou* is the world of time in which we live, and underneath is always the eternity rhythm, the *Ho-tou*. That idea underlay the whole cultural and scientific application of mathematics in China. Let us compare it with our viewpoint.

I want to read you in detail what the well-known mathematician, Hermann Weyl, says about it in his book *Philosophy of Mathematics and Natural Science*. You know that until about 1930 the great and passionate occupation of most mathematicians was the discussion of the fundamentals. They hoped, as has been the fashion nowadays, to rediscuss the fundamentals of all science. But the famous German mathematician, David Hilbert, created a new construction

14

of the whole building of mathematics, so to speak, and hoped that this would contain no internal contradictions. There would be a few basic axioms on which one could build up all branches of mathematics: topology, geometry, algebra, and so on; it was to be a big building with solid foundations in a few axioms. That was in 1926, and Hilbert was even bold enough to say: "I think that with my theory the discussion of fundamentals has been forever removed from mathematics."

Then in 1931 came another very famous mathematician, Kurt Goedel, who took a few of those basic axioms and showed that one could reach complete contradictions with them: starting from the same axioms, one could prove something and its complete opposite. In other words, he showed that the basic axioms contain an irrational factor which could not be eliminated. Nowadays in mathematics one must not say that obviously this is so-and-so, and that therefore that and that is also so, but: "I assume that it is so-and-so, and if so then that and that follows." The axioms must be presented as assumptions, or must be postulated, after which a logical deduction can be made, but one cannot infer that what has been assumed or postulated could not be contradicted or doubted as an absolute truth.

In order to make such assumptions, mathematics are generally formulated in such terms as: "It is self-evident," or "It is reasonable to think" — that is how mathematicians posit an axiom nowadays, and from there they build up. From then on there is no contradiction, only one conclusion is possible, but in "it is reasonable to assume," that is where the dog lies buried, as we say. Goedel showed that, and thus threw over the whole thing. Strangely enough that did not reopen the discussion of fundamentals. From then on, as Weyl says, nobody touched that problem, they just felt awkward and scratched behind their ears and said, "Don't let's discuss fundamentals, there's nothing doing: it is reasonable to assume, we cannot go beyond that," and there the situation rests today.

Weyl, however, went through a very interesting development. At first he was very much attracted by the physicist, Werner Heisenberg. He was very much of a Pythagorean and was attracted by the numinosity and irrationality of natural integers. Then he became fascinated by David Hilbert, and in the middle of his life had a period during which he became more and more attracted by Hilbertian logic and dropped the problem of numbers, treating them, er-

15

roneously as I think, as simply posited quantities. He says, for instance, that natural integers are just as though one took a stick and made a row of marks, which one then named conventionally; there was nothing more behind them, they were simply posited by the human mind and there was nothing mysterious about them; it was "reasonable and self-evident" that one could do that. But at the end of his life he added (only to the German edition of his book on the philosophy of mathematics, and shortly before his death) this passage:

> The beautiful hope we had of freeing the world of the discussion of fundamentals was destroyed by Kurt Goedel in 1931 and the ultimate basis and real meaning of mathematics are still an open problem. Perhaps one makes mathematics as one does music and it is just one of man's creative activities, and though the idea of an existing completely transcendental world is the basic principle of all formalism, each mathematical formalism has at every step the characteristics of being incomplete [which means that every mathematical theory is consistent in itself but is incomplete, at the borders are questions which are not self-evident, are not clear, and are incomplete] in so far as there are always problems, even of a simple arithmetical nature, which can be formulated in the frame of a formalism, but which cannot be decided by deduction within the formalism itself.

That is put in a mathematician's complicated way; put simply, it means that I daresay it is self-evident, by which I posit something irrational, because it is not self-evident. Now one could make an *uroboros* movement and say: "But from my deduction I can re-prove my beginning." You cannot! You cannot from the deductive formalism afterwards deduce a proof, except by a tautology, which naturally is not allowed, even in mathematics.

> We are therefore not surprised that in an isolated phenomenal existence a piece of nature surprises us by its irrationality and that one cannot analyse it completely. As we have seen, physics therefore projects everything which exists onto the background of possibility or probability.

That is important because it sums up in one word what modern science does. In other words, any fragment of phenomenal existence, let us say these spectacles, contains something irrational which one cannot exhaust in physical analysis. Why the electrons of these millions and millions of atoms of which my spectacles consist are in this place and not in another, I cannot explain; therefore through physics, when it comes to a single event in nature, there is no completely valid explanation.

16

The single event is always irrational, but in physics one proceeds by projecting this onto the background of a possible, i.e., one makes a matrix. For instance, in these spectacles there are so many atoms and so many particles of them, and so on, and out of a whole group one can make a mathematical formula in which one could even count the particles — not 1, 2, 3, 4, 5, but by projecting onto the background of what is possible. That is why these matrices are nowadays used in engineering and so on, because one can cope with the uncountable; they provide an instrument with which to cope with the things which cannot be counted singly. Weyl says:

> It is not surprising that any bit of nature we may choose [these spectacles or anything] has an ultimate irrational factor which we cannot and never will explain and that we can only describe it, as in physics, by projecting it onto the background of the possible.

But then he continues:

> But it is very surprising that something which the human mind has created itself, namely the series of whole natural integers [I told you that he has this erroneous idea that the human mind created 1, 2, 3, 4, 5, by making dots], and which is so absolutely simple and transparent to the constructive spirit, also contains an aspect of something abysmal which we cannot grasp.

That is the confession of one of the most remarkable — because one of the most philosophically oriented — modern mathematicians, Hermann Weyl. We can naturally say that we do not believe what he believed, namely that the natural integers simply represent the naming of posited dots, therefore to us it is not surprising that natural integers are abysmal and beyond our grasp. He believed that, and that is why he could not understand. It is incredible that it should be so, but it is so; in other words, because the natural integers have something irrational (he called it abysmal) the fundamentals of mathematics are not solid, because the whole of mathematics is ultimately based on the givenness of the series of natural integers.

Now precisely because numbers are irrational and abysmal — to quote Weyl — they are a good instrument with which to grasp something irrational. If one uses numbers to grasp the irrational, one uses irrational means to get hold of something irrational, and that is the basis of divination. They took those irrationl, abysmal numbers which nobody has so far understood, and tried to guess reality, or their connection with reality — but into the divination problem there also enters the problem of time.

17

Divination has to do with synchronicity, and Jung has in so many words called the synchronistic phenomena parapsychological phenomena. I want you to keep that in mind because, as you know, in modern science physicists and psychologists are now trying to find the union of physics and psychology in the area of parapsychological phenomena. They have a hunch, or guess, that parapsychological phenomena might give us a clue to the union of physis and psyche. Now in divination, and I am here referring specifically to number divination, one would therefore also have to deal with the parapsychological phenomenon, which at the same time is linked up with the number. Jung has called number the most primitive expression of the spirit and so we have now to go into what we understand, from the psychological standpoint, by the word spirit.

Jung, in trying to specify how he uses the word spirit, first quotes a lot of colloquial terms in which spirit is used as something like a non-material substance, or as the opposite of matter.* We also generally use the word spirit to indicate something that is a cosmic principle, but we use the same word when we speak of certain of man's psychological psychic capacities or activities like the intellect, or the capacity to think, or reason. For instance, one could say: "He has a spiritual outlook," or "This idea comes from a distorted spirit," or something like that. Again we use the word as a collective phenomenon such as in the word *Zeitgeist* which is now generally not even translated into English — it is a German term to express the irrational fact that each period of time has a certain spirit.

For instance, the Renaissance had a certain spirit as illustrated in its art, its technology, mathematics, and religious outlook everywhere. All these phenomena which characterize the 16th century could be summed up as the spirit of the Renaissance. In that sense the word is simply used as a collective phenomenon, the sum of ideas common to many people. One could also speak of the spirit of Marxism or of National Socialism, when it would be the common collective ideas of a whole group. There is therefore, Jung continues, a certain opposition between *a spirit*, which has a kind of extra-human existence outside man — the cosmic spirit as opposed to the matter of the cosmos — and something which we experience as

*Cf. "The Phenomenology of the Spirit in Fairytales," Collected Works, Vol. 9, I, pars. 384 ff.

an activity of the human ego. If we say of somebody that he has a distorted spirit, that means his ego complex is working intellectually in a wrong way. Jung therefore continues: If something psychic, or psychological (i.e., a psychological event) happens in the individual and he has the feeling that it belongs to him, then he calls it his spirit for instance – which, by the way, would be quite wrong, but which many people do. If I suddenly had the idea of giving you a good example, then I would feel that it was my good idea, my spirit produced it. If something psychological happens which seems strange to the individual, then it is called a spirit, in the sense of something like a ghost, and then one experiences it as possession.

Let us assume that suddenly I felt impelled to keep saying, "the geraniums are blue," "the geraniums are blue," "the geraniums are blue." Then, because that would be crazy, and seem to me quite strange compared with what I am now doing here, I would say: "My God, what devil, or ghost, put such a crazy idea into my head, it is possessing me and making me talk nonsense!" If it were a good idea then I'd follow it right through! Now primitives are more honest: everything which comes to them unexpectedly from within they call spirit; not only that which is bad and which possesses one, but anything of which they would say: "My ego did not make it, it suddenly came to me" – that is spirit. In the latter case, when the spirit is still outside, when I get possessed by having to say or do something which seems not to belong to my ego, then it is a projected aspect of my unconscious; it is a part of my unconscious psyche which is projected and then experienced as a parapsychological phenomenon.

That happens when you get into a state in which you are not yourself, or into an emotional upset where you lose control of yourself, but afterwards wake up completely sober and look at the stupid things you did during your possessed state and wonder what got into you: something got hold of you, you weren't yourself, though while you were behaving like that you thought you were – it was just as if an evil spirit or the devil had got into you.

These things one must not just take in a kind of colloquial amusing way, but quite literally, for a devil – or we would say, more neutrally, an autonomous complex – temporarily replaces the ego complex; it feels like the ego at the time, but it isn't, for afterwards, when dissociated from it, one cannot understand how one came to do or think such things.

19

One of the main ways in which we use the word spirit is in speaking of the inspiring, vivifying aspect of the unconscious. Now we know that for the ego complex to get in touch with the unconscious has a vivifying and inspiring effect, and that is really the basis of all our therapeutic efforts. Sometimes neurotic people, who have become closed up in their neurotic vicious circle, as soon as they go into analysis and have dreams, get excited and interested in the dreams and then the water of life flows again; they once more have an interest and therefore are suddenly more alive and more efficient. Then somebody may say: "What has happened to you? You have come alive again" — but that only happens if the individual succeeds in making contact with the unconscious, or one could say "with the dynamism of the unconscious," and especially with its vivifying, inspiring aspect.

Jung therefore defines spirit, from the psychological angle, as *the dynamic aspect of the unconscious*. One can think of the unconscious as being like still water, a lake which is passive. The things one forgets fall into that lake; if one remembers them one fishes them up but it itself does not move. The unconscious has that matrix, womb aspect, but it also has the aspect of containing dynamism and movement, it acts on its own accord — for instance, it composes dreams. One could say that composing dreams while one sleeps is an aspect of the spirit; some master spirit or mind composes a most ingenious series of pictures which, if one can decipher them, seem to convey a highly intelligent message. That is a dynamic manifestation of the unconscious, where the unconscious energetically does something on its own, it moves and creates on its own, and that is what Jung defines as spirit. There is naturally an unclear borderline between the subjective and the objective; but in practice if one feels that it belongs to one then it is one's own spirit, and if one does not feel it belongs to one, then one calls it *the* spirit, or *a* spirit. That depends on whether one feels akin or not akin to it, close to it or not close to it.

Jung sums up by saying that spirit contains a spontaneous psychic principle of movement and activity; secondly, that it has the quality of freely creating images beyond our sense perception (in a dream one has no sense perception — the spirit or the unconscious creates images from within, while the sense perceptions are asleep); and thirdly, there is an autonomous and sovereign manipulation of those images.

Those are the three characteristics of what Jung calls the spirit, or the dynamism of the unconscious. It is spontaneously active, it freely creates images beyond sensual perceptions, and it autonomously and in a sovereign manner manipulates those images. If one looks at one's dreams, one sees that they are composed of impressions from the day before. For instance, one read something in a paper, or experienced something in the street, or talked to Mrs. So-and-So, and so on. The dream takes these fragments and makes a completely new and meaningful potpourri out of that. There one sees the sovereign manipulation of the pictures: they are put into another order and manipulated into a completely different sequence with a completely different meaning, though one still recognizes that the single elements have been taken from, for instance, memory remnants of the day before. That is why many people think that is the whole explanation of the dream: "Oh, I read about a fire yesterday in the paper, that is why I dreamt about a fire," and then one has to begin, as always, by saying: "Yes, but look at the connections in which the fire has been put, very different from what you read." That would be the spirit, that unknown thing in the unconscious which rearranges and manipulates inner images.

This factor which produces and manipulates inner images is completely autonomous in primitive man, but through the differentiation of consciousness it slowly comes closer to consciousness, and therefore in contrast to primitives we say we do it in part. For instance, we often say that we have a good idea or we invent something new. A primitive man would never say that a bow and arrow, for instance, were his invention — he would say that the way to construct a bow and arrow was revealed to him by the bow and arrow god, and then tell an origin myth, of how to a certain hunter his divinity appeared in a dream or vision and revealed to him how to make a bow and arrow.

So the larger our consciousness is, and the more it develops, the more we get hold of certain aspects of the spirit of the unconscious, draw it into our subjective sphere, and then call it our own psychic activity or our own spirit. But, as Jung points out, a great part of the original phenomenon remains naturally autonomous and therefore still is experienced as a parapsychological phenomenon. In other words, we must not assume that at our present stage of consciousness, where we have assimilated more than a certain amount

21

of the spirit of the unconscious and made it our own — i.e., made it the possession of the ego complex so that the ego complex can manipulate it — that we have the whole thing. There is still an enormous area of that spirit which manifests as it did originally, completely autonomously, and therefore as a parapsychological phenomenon, as it does among primitive people.

If one looks at the history of mathematics one can see very clearly how the spirit becomes subjective. For instance, the natural integers or numbers, as you probably all know, were for the Pythagoreans cosmic divine principles which constituted the basic structure of the universe. They were gods, divinities, and at the same time the basic structural principle of all existence. Even Leopold Kronecker still said that the natural numbers were the invention of the Godhead and that everything else was man's handiwork.

Nowadays, in this time of so-called enlightenment where everything irrational and the word God anyhow is thrown out of human science, a real attempt has been made in formalistic mathematics to define number in a form which would exclude all irrational elements, with the definition of numbers as a series of marks (1, 2, 3, 4, 5) and a creation of the human mind. Now the spirit is seemingly owned by the ego complex, the mathematician's ego owns and created numbers! That is what Weyl believed, and that is why he said: "I cannot understand that something completely simple which the human mind has created suddenly contains something abysmal." He should only have asked whether the human mind had really created them. He feels as if he were now manipulating the phenomenon completely, but that is not true.

Primitives, if they have twenty horses, cannot count the horses themselves but they use twenty sticks and then they say, one stick, one horse, two sticks, two horses, three sticks, three horses, and then they count the sticks and with them they can count the number of horses. That is a very, very widespread way in which man learned to count. We still do it on our fingers — if somebody enumerates things, we point to our fingers, using them as a "helping quantity." All counting began with the helping quantity. When man first could count something and then had to count more, he used his fingers; or in many, many primitive civilizations they use dots or counting sticks and then when something has to be counted sticks are put down and counted and that is the helping quantity.

Thus if we do what Hermann Weyl did we simply go back to that primitive way, we count the helping quantity; but that is only an action of the human mind, not the numbers themselves. To make such helping sticks or dots is an activity of ego consciousness by which one can count; it is a construction of the human mind but the number itself is *not*, and there is the great error.

So we have to turn back and say, Yes, numbers have an aspect in which they are entities which the human mind can posit and manipulate. We can assume a certain amount of numbers, an arithmetical law, a situation, and that can be manipulated completely freely and arbitrarily, according to our ego wishes, *but* we manipulate only the derivative; the original thing which inspired one to make counting sticks and so arrive at the number of horses, for instance, that idea one has not got hold of, it is still autonomous, it still belongs to the creative spirit of the unconscious, so to speak.

At the time of Weyl, therefore, one simply discarded the study of single numbers because one always stumbled over something completely simple and queer: one had just posited four dots, and then suddenly those four dots developed qualities which one had not posited. In order to get away from that awkward situation and keep up the illusion that numbers were something one had posited and could manipulate with one's conscious mind, Weyl says: "The single numbers are not emphasized in mathematics but one projects them by a specific procedure onto the background of infinite possibilities and then copes with them that way."

That is what most modern mathematicians do. They simply take the theory of natural integers, from one to N, and cope with it as a whole; they say simply that is the series of natural integers which has certain qualities — for instance every number has a predecessor, a successor, a position, and a ratio. One knows that as a whole, and then one can construct other mathematics with complex and irrational numbers, etc. One then derives much higher forms, always of types (one could say of numbers), and one deals with that simply as what the mathematician calls a *class*, ignoring the seven, the fifteen and the 335 in it.

Therefore one deals with an algebraic idea and only with those qualities which are common to all natural integers. With those one can build a lot, but more or less, as Weyl says, "ignore the single integer." Mathematicians are very honest people; they never deny that the single number has irrational, individual qualities, they are simply not interested. Poincaré, for instance, is even more honest, he says that all natural integers are irrational individuals, but that is exactly why one cannot make many general theories in number theory about them, and why they are not very prolific for mathematics. They are not very useful, because there are too many single cases and not enough generalities from which one can make a theorem. That was Poincaré's viewpoint, he did not say it was not interesting, but that we do not like it so much because one cannot make theorems out of it. We would have to pay attention to the single case and that we do not like as mathematicians, because temperamentally we prefer to make general theories which are generally valid.

Therefore in the history of mathematics one can very clearly see what Jung characterized as the general development of the human mind: that anything which we now call our subjective spirit, including our mental activities in science, was once the objective spirit — that means the inspiring movement of the unconscious psyche — but with the development of consciousness, we have got hold of a part that we now manipulate and call our own, behaving as if it were something which we completely possess. That has happened in the whole development of mathematics: from numbers being gods, they have been desecrated into being something which is arbitrarily posited by a mathematician's ego. But the mathematicians are honest enough to say: "No, that is not the whole of it, strangely enough there are things which I wanted and have had which still slip and do things which they ought not to do, they have not become the slaves of our consciousness completely."

A parallel development has happened in the history of physics where now, more and more, the concept of probability is used and one tries to ignore as much as possible the single case. Wolfgang Pauli therefore said: "Because of the indeterministic character of natural law, physical observation acquires the character of an irrational unique actuality and a result you cannot predict; against it stands the rational aspect of an abstract order of possibility which one posits with the help of the mathematical concept of probability and the *psi* function."

In other words, physics is now confronted with a great split, namely all the pre-calculations are based on the concept of probability and are calculated in matrix and other algebraic forms, but with them one can only state a general probability. Then one makes an actual observation which is a unique actual event. Now these actual unique observations, even if they cost ten million dollars, for instance — and they do nowadays in the realm of microphysics — one cannot repeat infinitely so as also to get a certain practical probability. There is therefore an immense gap, and that is why Pauli says the actual experiment (let's say with a particle in a cyclotron) is an irrational "just-so story" which generally does not quite fit the calculated probability. That is why nowadays one fudges all those equations in physics; in fact one just cheats a bit to bind them to each other, and one cannot make actual accurate predictions any more.

Naturally, physicists have thought about that! How does that happen? Why can one not make an actual prediction which should really give actual numerical results, not only a statistical probability? Pauli very clearly states that it comes from the presuppositions, because the experiment is an actual single event and the means of calculation in mathematics are based on the principle of probability, which excludes, and does not apply to, the unique event.

Therefore we now have to go deeper into the problem of probability and say: "How does that happen?" The simplest way of explaining probabilities, and the way I am going to use because it is apparently the archetypal pattern, is with cards. One has a set of 32 cards and may pick one card. The probability that out of the 32 cards one gets, say, the Ace of Hearts, is one-thirtysecond. One has just that much chance and no more. If I say you may pick ten times, then naturally the probability of getting the Ace of Hearts is much better, and if you may pick a thousand times then the chance becomes still better, and so on.

In other words repetition is the secret of probability: the more one repeats the situation, the more accurately the probability can be formulated, till finally, and that is the statistical formulation, one gets to a limit value where one can say that when one has N (that means an infinite number of draws) then a limit can be made pretty accurately. That, in popularized, simplified form, is what underlies calculable probability.

Not being a mathematician and physicist I had generally to rely on rather popularized material and there the physicist, when he wants to explain probability, always uses the example either of dice or cards. Just keep that in mind. If he explains the theorem of Bernoulli he begins by saying, "Well you see if you have so and so many cards," and so on. The same way is always used to explain probability to a lay person. But why just that example? That is amusing! But to go now to the fact, it means that all mathematics, and their use in modern physics, are based on the principle of admitting an inability to make single predictions of single events, but aiming at being able to do so when it comes into thousands and billions of events which then gain a great amount of accuracy.

Now, as a wicked psychologist, and not believing in this, or rather seeing this as a very one-sided operation of the human mind, one has to ask two questions: first, naturally, one sees oneself that it is a very questionable or a very one-sided grasp of reality which modern science gets by applying these techniques, and therefore one is justified in asking if there are not other possibilities with other means. For the moment, however, I want to ask the other question: "Why on earth did millions of highly intelligent scientists in Western Europe and America and the Western world believe in the law of great numbers as if it were God?" Because, actually, if one discusses these problems with modern natural scientists they just believe this is it — that it is our way of getting at reality and describing it scientifically and accurately. There is the implication that this is where one gets at the truth of inner and outer factors and everything else; it must be statistically proved and it must cover itself with this concept of probability.

That is my great criticism of Rhine of Duke University. Even he was foolish enough to believe that if he wanted to sell parapsychological phenomena to the scientific world then he must prove them statistically or with the concept of probability and — what a fool — he ended up by that in enemy territory. He should have stayed on his own territory. He tries to prove with the very means which eliminates the single case, something which is only valid in the single case. That is why I do not believe in that whole investigation. I do not believe in what they do in Duke University. They became seduced by the *Zeitgeist* of America, and because they wanted to prove to other scientists that their parapsychology is real science they used a tool which is absolutely inept and inadequate for the purpose. That is my personal view.

Let us now first ask why that mania of believing in the law of great numbers has possessed the Western mind? After all, those who believe in it are, in the main, the most developed and intelligent people in our civilization. They are not fools. Now why do they believe in it? If somebody believes, as a kind of holy conviction, something which after one has woken up about it proves to be a very partial and partly an erroneous viewpoint, then the psychological suspicion always exists that these people are under the secret influence of an archetype. *That is what makes people believe things which are not true.*

26

If one looks at the history of science one sees that all the errors in science, or what we now call errors, have been due to the fact that people in the past were fascinated by an archetypal idea which prevented them from observing facts further. That archetypal concept satisfied them, it gave them a subjective feeling of "this is it" and therefore they gave up looking for further explanations. Only when a scientist came along and said, "Now I am not so sure of that," and brought new facts did they wake up and ask: "Why on earth did we believe that other story before, it appears now to be erroneous!" Generally one sees that one was under the spell, the emotional, fascinating spell of an archetypal idea.

We have therefore to ask what archetypal idea is behind the spell which now grips the minds of modern scientists? Who is the lord of great numbers, seen from a mythological standpoint? If one studies the history of religion and comparative mythology the only beings who ever were able to manipulate great numbers were gods, or the godhead. God, even in the Old Testament, counted the hairs of our head. We cannot do that, but He can. Moreover, the Jews refused to be counted because only God was allowed to know the number of His people and to count the population was sacrilege — only the Divinity could count.

Most primitive societies that still live in the aboriginal state of the collector and hunter type, for instance the Australian aborigines, all have a binary system. They count to two and then they count on in couples. They have no word beyond two, they count one, two; two, one, two; two, two, one, one, two, and so on. In most primitive civilizations they can either count to two, or to three, or to four. There are different types and beyond a certain number they say "many," and where many begins there begins the irrational, the godhead.

There one sees how man, in learning to count, took away a little bit of territory from that all-counting god, just a little bit, the one and the two; that is what he can manage, the rest still belongs to the all-counting god. In counting to three and then four and then five, he slowly gains territory, but there always comes the moment when he says "many," and there he gives up counting; there "the other" counts, namely the unconscious (or the archetype, or the godhead), which can count infinitely, and can out-count every computer.

That is the fascination and I will go on from there next time.

27

Lecture 2

I tried last time to give you a short sketch of the basis of the calculus of probability and its use in modern physics and other fields of modern science. I tried to show you that the calculus of probability and the statistical methods used in modern science are only abstractions founded on the idea of the infinite series of natural integers, and that they gain in accuracy only if you assume an infinite number of events or examples.

Dr. Jung always exemplified this by saying that if you had a heap of stones, you could with absolute statistical accuracy say that their average size was, let us say, three cubic centimeters, but if you wanted to pick *one* stone of exactly that size you would have great trouble; you might find one, or perhaps even none. In other words, though the statement that the average size of the stones in the heap is three cubic centimeters is true, it is an abstraction in our minds. We make this abstraction in our minds which is accurate as far as it is true, but the reality in the heap of stones where each stone is different is not like that. Most people, if one tells them with a certain conviction that the average man, or the average American, is so and so, believe it; they believe it as if the real Americans, or the real stones, were like that. They make that error though they must also know that it is a mental abstraction, for the actual accumulation of people is an accumulation of unique cases.

This abstraction has proved very helpful, which is one of the reasons why people believe it, but it is not the whole reason, because if one argues with natural scientists they brush aside the fact that the actual stones are of different size, they won't hear about that. Those who are honest say, "That does not concern science," the unique or the individual case does not concern science, because

28

so far there are no mathematical means of getting at it. Most people believe, and it is an emotional conviction, that statistical truth is *the* truth. In discussions, therefore, they always give this kind of an answer: "It has been statistically proved to be so, and that is sufficient," and there the discussion ends.

Now if people believe something which is obviously stupid — I should not really call it stupid, but one-sided, for it is a one-sided view of the world — an abstraction which people believe as if it were the gospel truth, then, as a psychologist, one has always to ask why. What causes this emotion, why can one not discuss with other people, why can they not see such an obvious truth? For instance, as I just tried to show you with a heap of stones, naturally they are unique stones, why do they either get emotional and say the unique stone does not exist, or that it exists but that that has nothing to do with science?

At first I used to just get irritated with such scientists, but then I reminded myself that I was a psychologist, so had better see why they were so emotionally tied to the idea that the calculus of probability or statistics is the truth, and that there is no other. By going back and looking at the origin, one sees that at the back of this belief is the working of an archetype. If people cannot discuss things in a detached way and relatively truthfully, it is because they are influenced by an archetype. I therefore asked myself what was the archetypal image behind the idea of an infinite series of integers $(1, 2, 3, \ldots$ etc.$)$. Why was the calculus of probability operated with this magnitude, or this quantum, so to speak, as if it were a whole? There one finds that mankind — and that was where I stopped last time — has slowly learnt to count. The most primitive peoples, for instance certain Australian aborigines, can only count to two in words, afterwards they repeat and count in couples. They have a so-called binary system. Other primitive people can count to three, after which they say "many"; others can count to five and then say "many," or they begin to repeat.

Counting probably originated first with the use of reckoning aids, either pebbles or sticks. When one could not count all the objects one always used the counting pebble by which to make a one-to-one relationship. The pebbles are a way for human consciousness to get hold of number, so some can count to three and some to four, after which they generally say "many," or they shrug their shoulders; then comes the concept of the group, the class of natural integers, in which one cannot realize the single individual. In that way they all have this concept of an infinite number of natural integers generally covered by the word "many," but now who handles the many?

> *Infinite series of integers:*
> 1, 2, 3 . . . many . . . N (the godhead).
> N - the group or class of natural integers.

Nowadays we can handle it, we can handle the many as if it were a magnitude, something one can use in mathematics. Primitive man assumes that only a god or a godhead can count infinitely. He owns, so to speak, the awareness — the depreciated awareness — of this number N, while for modern mankind that would be inhuman. Man owns three or twenty, or however far he can count, and then comes the archetype of the N and that is in the hands of a godhead. There are different gods who can count in this form. In the New Testament it is said that God counted the hairs of our heads (Luke 12:7); but there are also negative godheads, for other gods can count, not only the supreme God of the New Testament. For instance, the West African tribe of the Yoruba have the following prayer:

> *Death:* Counting, counting, counting continually, does not count me;
> *Fire:* counting continually, counting continually, does not count me;
> *Emptiness:* counting continually, counting continually, does not count me;
> *Wealth:* counting continually, counting continually, does not count me;
> *Day:* counting continually, counting continually, does not count me;
> The spider's web is round the cornbin.

(I have not repeated the "counting continually" as often as they do.) "The spider's web is round the cornbin" is a very mysterious saying. The ethnologist from whose report I quote this prayer says it is not quite explained, and that there is a variation of the last sentence which goes, "Soot is round the cornbin." He thinks it might be that they put soot round the cornbin to prevent theft, and also to have the traces if there was theft, so a ring of soot would be a protection for the cornbin. The spider's web is probably the same thing for if that is unbroken, then nobody has touched the cornbin. But naturally we would also think of the fact that the spider's web is a beautiful, ordered mandala, so it would mean that there is a secret order which protects one's own possessions.

30

For me the important part of this prayer is that it addresses Death, Fire, Emptiness, Wealth, and Day — five archetypal powers which can count. The connotations are obvious. Death always counts, and it is very unfortunate if it gets our number, for then Death has us. Death perpetually takes away from mankind and apparently does it consciously, knowing that now So-and-So and So-and-So have to leave the living. Fire constantly consumes, spreads, and burns; it always needs more fuel, so fire consumes more and more, as does death. Emptiness is also an archetypal power; in all primitive and antique creation myths, at the beginning of the world there is either a godhead or emptiness — the Void, so to speak, and the Void one could call a creative potentiality, it is the "not yet being." — that too is an image for the unconscious, that too can count. Wealth counts, that's obvious, everybody knows that wealthy people count their money, or that's how the greedy see it, not so untruly. And Day, the principle of consciousness, or the period of consciousness, can also count.

All these things — death, fire, emptiness, wealth, and day — are images of what we would call psychic energy as the source of consciousness. Fire and wealth are obvious symbols for psychic energy. Then one thinks of the old descriptions of the godhead of death, as for instance in the Graeco-Roman religion where Death is Jupiter or Zeus of the Underworld, the god of the infinite and the treasure keeper. The land of the dead is like a treasury and the god of death like the keeper of an enormous treasury from which he reproduces the living and brings back dying people. He too, therefore, is the treasurer of life's energy and he, by means of numbers, by counting, produces it or takes it back again. Day, naturally, is symbolic, it is identical with the time of conscious awareness, in contrast to the night.

The Yoruba fear this god of the unconscious, and attribute to it the demonic capacity of counting. Their wish is *not* to be counted, to escape into the night of life, to escape this all-seeing eye of the godhead who distributes negative fate.

If we try to interpret this archetypal picture we could say that the image of the godhead, or of a great god — they are all images of the Self in our language — involves a numerically ordered rhythm, as if the Self were like a clock which pulses rhythmically: one, two, three, death, and one, two, three — and then it hits, or does not hit one. In its positive aspect it produces life and time, and in its negative aspect it is the all-consuming fire and death. One has the idea

31

that death is the counting power, the divine power. In the English language there is the expression, "His number was up." If somebody dies, not before the right time, and if one wants to express the feeling that that person died in harmony with his fate, then one says, "Oh well, his number was up," as a comfort, meaning that he did not die by accident before his time.

In religious language one could say that God had decided to kill that person now and nothing would have helped, even doctors could not have helped because Fate or God intended the person to die — God puts a number up and the person called has to go. So here there is an identity between an individual number and a human being; numbers are in that way individuals. Another English expression also expresses the fact that a number is like an individual and vice versa: if we do not understand somebody, we say we have not got his number, meaning we have not the frequency or the radar beam, or whatever it is, to get in touch with that personality. There too each individual has one frequency or one number, and in order to get in touch with that individual we have to have the right number.

Thus if nowadays man believes that he can handle an infinite series of natural numbers, that is an inflation, an identification with the archetype of the Self, or of the godhead. That was the fatal deed of a man called George Cantor, who first discovered that there are different infinities, or blocks, which one can add and subtract, and so on, and different powers of infiniteness, which one can count simultaneously or singly. Some are more and some less powerful, but the fatal thing is that Cantor thus introduced the illusion that by counting such a block number and then handling it mathematically one had it in hand, so to speak. We make the same fatal mistake when we think that a statistical truth is *the* truth, for we are really only handling an abstract concept and not reality itself, and into that thought then sneaks identification with the godhead. There is a Navaho myth which exemplifies what happens there, but in the form of play, so I must first go back to something else. Please keep in mind that I am going to try to show that it is an inflation. First, however, I want to explain another aspect.

The calculus of probability was invented by two great men: the French mathematician and philosopher Blaise Pascal, and another Frenchman who was really the greatest mathematician of all time, Pierre de Fermat. A gambler wrote to Pascal and asked him about a system for gambling. That now plays a great role, especially in Italy, where the *sistematici* play a role in the state lottery. Naturally when gifted mathematicians go to Monte Carlo, etc., many of them have systems, so this gambler asked Pascal to find one by which he could win. Pascal became mathematically interested and started a correspondence with Fermat about it. One cannot quite say who had the idea first, but in the back and forth of this correspondence between them they discovered the calculus of probability. Thus the actual historical root of probability is gambling. Remember I told you last lecture that whenever physicists or mathematicians try to explain in a popular form the calculus of probability, or the principles of statistics, they fall back on the idea of gambling. This suggests that the archetypal root is the archetype of the gambler and gambling. Now listen to the Navaho story.

The Navahos once had a very outstanding chief who owned all the pearls and treasures of the tribe and in order to be protected lived in seclusion. He had a big turquoise of which the Sungod was jealous. Though the Sungod himself also had a complete, or perfect turquoise, he wanted the chief's too. He therefore generated a son with Rock Woman and educated this son so that he should become a perfect gambler, one who always won. He then sent him down to earth to challenge the chief and win everything from him, including the great turquoise. This the son did. The Sungod then asked to have the turquoise, but his son, the Navaho gambler, kept it for himself. The Sungod was very angry and repeated the same performance. He again generated a son with Rock Woman and taught this one too, but the second son he also taught to cheat, with the help of animals.

In North American Indian and in Mayan mythology that plays a great role; the animals interfere and help the people who are in the right. For instance, there is the famous "Book of Counsel," the Popul-Vuh of the Quiché Maya, where the heroes have to fight the gods of the underworld who killed their fathers, and play a basketball kind of game which they could not win, because the gods of the underworld are more powerful. But at a certain moment a little rabbit runs into the goal as though it were the ball, and people mistake it, and everybody thinks that the heroes, and not the gods of the underworld, have won. They won with the help of the rabbit which cheated, and so they may behead the gods of the underworld and revenge their fathers.

Here the same thing happens, for the second gambler challenges the first gambler and, with the help of the animals — it is not specified in what way — he wins everything back from the first gambler. He then hands the great turquoise to his father, the Sungod, who rewards him by giving him great power and the possession of much land.

If we interpret this myth psychologically, the Sungod would be a parallel to Day, Death, Fire, and Emptiness in the Yoruba prayer; he is the god of the principle of consciousness in the unconscious. Or you could also call him the light of nature, the *lumen naturae*, and he therefore can count infinitely and he in *his* consciousness is aware of all gambling. Then he creates human consciousness, the first gambler, and teaches him his tricks. But the first gambler falls into an inflation, and after he has learnt the tricks from the Sungod he does not give back what the Sungod wants, as a sacrifice or as a reward for having taught him the tricks. He is an inflated hero, and therefore is doomed, because the Sungod then creates a second gambler who is human and modest, and honest enough to give back the great turquoise to the Sungod, knowing that he had only won through having learnt the Sungod's tricks and with the help of the animals, which here is the decisive factor. We would say that he remains true to his instinct, and does not become inflated.

Falling into an inflation means a betrayal of one's instincts. The instinct protects — we have an instinctual protection against inflation. We have all often become inflated and know that when one is inflated one feels uneasy. Even before we fall down the stairs we have the feeling that today we will fall down, because somehow we have a kind of bad conscience or malaise, we don't know why, and then — bump! — the punishment for inflation generally comes quickly; one walks into a car, or something like that.

We can therefore say that those people who nowadays do not reasonably appreciate the calculus of probability and statistics as useful and reasonable tools of the human mind, but who believe secretly that we can master nature and find *the* truth about everything, have fallen into such an inflation, into a secret identification with the Sungod. They are therefore punished by inflation. What is worse, inflation always means sterilization of the mind, for if one is inflated one is both sterile and stupid, and that, to a great extent, is the situation of modern natural science. I will not say that all are like that. There are many outstanding scientists with whom one can discuss these facts, and who are fully aware that through statistics and the calculus of probability we only reconstruct an abstract model of nature in our minds, and that that does not cover the whole reality, i.e., we have only useful partial knowledge, and there are still an infinite number of secrets, and an infinite number of other possible ways in which to explore reality.

Through George Cantor such an inflation entered the field of mathematics, as seen in the way mathematicians now handle their quantity of N, the infinite amount. This falling apart between handling possible infinity as if it were a unit, in contrast to the single natural integer, is a split in modern mathematical thinking, and the same split exists between the scientific experiment and the oracle of divination. Now — as you see — I am slowly working my way to my theme of divination.

Let me just characterize what I mean by an oracle of divination. For the moment I mean any human actions handling a numerical oracle. Afterwards I shall expand to others, but at first I will remain with number oracles.

A number is produced by some arbitrary gesture, for instance, by putting one's hand into a bowl of pebbles and taking some out and then counting them. Or by taking a number of chicken bones, making two sections in the sand, and then throwing the bones at random, afterwards counting how many fell into the red and how many into the white section, or something like that. Or probably most of you are familiar with the I Ching, for which one throws coins which fall heads or tails and one calculates from that, or one throws yarrow stalks, to get information about one's psycho-physical inner and outer situation.

Now this is a historical age-old first step by mankind to produce what one would call a system by which to investigate reality. Probably primitive man before he invented oracles relied only on his dreams and his instinctual unconscious hunches.

There is, for instance, a North American Indian tribe of the Naskapi Indians who live at the border, near the Alaskan Eskimos. There are only about one or two hundred people left, for they are rapidly starving to death. They live mainly on caribou fat. These people mirror a specifically primitive state of affairs. According to anthropological theories, and I must say I agree with such theories in this respect, we can say that they still mirror a very original state of mankind. Little scattered groups, usually family groups of about fifteen to twenty individuals, wander about in bands, the men hunting and the women collecting berries, etc. They have no agriculture and no civilization and are still completely the original hunter-collector type. Once a year the whole tribe meets at a certain place to sell furs and get munitions from the white man. Otherwise they never meet together, so have no organized religion, no festivals, and no priests, nothing. Since religion is a natural instinctual phenomenon, naturally they have one, though not organized, and for their spiritual orientation they rely on their dreams.

Their interpretation is that in the heart of every man dwells Mistap'eo, the great man who is the sender of dreams. He sends dreams and wants the individual to attend to those dreams, to test them, try them out, and draw their conclusions from them. They say that Mistap'eo also likes it very much if one draws or paints one's dream motifs, so they cut them in wood or they make little bark trays with dream motifs, and with that they have their spiritual orientation. They also sometimes discuss their dreams with one another and if a man or woman has a very impressive dream they spontaneously turn it into a song. If one man has a very good dream song then the others begin to sing it too, but even those songs fade out after a while, and then there is a new song from another individual who has transformed his dream into a song. Such songs are completely primitive. I can give you an example.

A man once dreamt that his wife was sleeping with a stranger. Now, like the Eskimos, they have a custom that if a stranger comes they offer their wives to him for the first night; it is the *ius primae noctis* in a certain variation. Psychologically, the stranger is a dangerous intruder, something of which the primitive man is always terrified. What will he bring? Will he integrate our life? Their fear is reinforced by the fact that often whites or other strangers bring a new disease. Not long ago these people had an awful wave of flu; one man caught it from the whites and infected the others, and since they have no immunity against flu half the tribe died. That is something which has happened to many Eskimo tribes, as you know. Therefore, their experience is that a stranger is a physiological and psychological threat which they try to meet by offering their wives. There is the feeling that he has thus become one of the family and therefore cannot do any harm, but is now propitious.

So a Naskapi man once dreamt that his wife was sleeping with a stranger. On waking up he thought about that and said: "Ha, today

I shall shoot a caribou!" Frank Speck, the ethnologist who tells the story, unfortunately does not say how he arrived at that conclusion. He didn't squeeze the man and enquire, but if you are primitive enough you will see at once how he did it: namely that something new would intrude into his life and his wife would sleep with it, therefore it must be something positive and not something dangerous — so something positive and new was to happen that day.

Since he was nearly starving, the only positive new thing which could happen would be to get a caribou which would mean survival for the next fortnight. Those people live from fortnight to fortnight. They reckon constantly with death, and live from each bear and each caribou they have killed; the situation is as bad as that and so: "I am going to shoot a caribou." He did shoot one and made a song: "My wife is sleeping with a stranger and I am going to shoot a caribou." That was a magical song imitated by many, many others of the tribe for a long time to provoke the situation of shooting a caribou, while originally it was just a psychological event, a dream of one Naskapi Indian.

That is probably how man oriented himself originally, before he invented oracles, for the invention of oracles would imply a further progress and is the beginning of science since it poses the question of how these probabilities could be systematized in some form. If I dream that my wife sleeps with a stranger then there is the probability that I shall shoot a caribou! That was how the tribe understood it. Now if they evolved culturally, which they do not — though we must assume that that has happened somewhere in the world at one time — then they would, for instance, try to sculpt a caribou and sing the song hoping that would magically result in the shooting of a caribou. That is hunting magic; it is not yet using an oracle, but those people know even hunting magic sometimes works and sometimes does not.

People who live on the level of the magic view of the world never believe that magic is like an absolute law; they will say they perform their hunting ritual, or hunting or some other magic, because of the hope and probability that it will come off, but though there is a strong probability of success it might not come off and they would explain that by saying some evil powers had interfered. If it does not work, they explain it by saying that an evil sorcerer has used some negative magic and disturbed the process, or they take it upon themselves and say they have not done the magical ritual

37

with quite the right psychological attitude, and then it sometimes does not work. So they reckon with failure: it is only a probability, not an absolute natural law.

Therefore let us assume that they carve a caribou in wood and make some magic with it, singing the song, after which sometimes they shoot a caribou and sometimes they do not. For the searching human mind then comes the next step: Could we find some means of knowing ahead if it will work or not?

Now there the concept of chance is introduced; to a certain extent it is a question of luck, or of chance, which for the primitive man means the action of a god, or a sorcerer, or one's own psychic powers — they do sometimes fail and therefore could they not find out ahead? One could, for instance (I am jumping now) throw a coin, and if the coin falls wrong then *I* am wrong, or the gods are not willing to help, and even if I use my hunting magic now it will not help. That is a short cut which saves me from exerting myself in drawing or dancing; I know ahead that the odds are against me, so I can save my energy and try to circumvent my bad luck in some other way. That would be the first dim dawning of a scientific mind. It consists in counting probabilities, in using some mathematical or other means to establish probabilities, and by that save energy and get the dark situation in which man lives in nature a bit more under his control. That is probably the origin of many, many oracle techniques which exist all over the world.

Now I come to the difference between a number oracle and another divination technique. There are innumerable divination techniques which to my mind are techniques to catalyze one's own unconscious knowledge. These do not use number, but some chaotic pattern; still much used among white men are tea leaves and coffee grounds, but you can use any other such pattern. As I told you before, there is an African technique of divination in which after eating a chicken its bones are thrown on the ground and from the way they fall, the chaotic pattern they make, may be read what is going to happen.

There is a village in the Swiss canton of Uri where church and cemetery are on the other side of a little river, so for a funeral they have to carry the coffin over the bridge to the church and cemetery. A dry mud path leads towards the bridge; in good weather it has cracks, and all the village people still look at those cracks nowadays as they follow the coffin, and by them can tell who will be the next, by looking at that chaotic pattern of cracks in the dry mud.

38

Once many years ago I consulted a palmist named Spier, a Dutchman who wrote a famous scientific book on palmistry. He had an enormous scientific apparatus and knew all the various lines in the hand. He didn't look at your hand but put soot on it, and then you had to make an imprint on paper and he read from that. He was a fantastic medium. I did not let him tell me my future; I thought I owned my own future and that was none of his business, so I bound him down only to tell me my past. He told it most accurately; he even saw an operation I had had two years before — and he didn't say some accident, he said an operation. He was just fantastic. So then I got interested and had coffee with him and squeezed him and asked him exactly how he did it. Finally he confessed, he told me that he was a medium and that when a person came into the room to consult him, he knew all about him; he just knew it, but did not know *what* he knew, and this whole performance with the cracks and the handlines was to bring up the knowledge he had. In that way he could project his unconscious knowledge into these lines and inform his client, so they were a catalyzer to make him conscious of what he already knew. Really, he drew on what Jung calls the absolute knowledge of the unconscious, which we know exists, as we can see from dreams.

The unconscious *knows* things; it knows the past and future, it knows things about other people. We all from time to time have dreams which inform us about something which happens to another person. Most of you who analyse will know that prognostic and telepathic dreams occur quite frequently to practically everybody, and this knowledge of the unconscious Jung calls absolute knowledge. A medium is a person who has a closer relationship, one might say a gift, by which to relate to the absolute knowledge of the unconscious, generally by having a relatively low level of consciousness. This explains why mediums are very often very queer and often even morally odd people — not always, but often — or they are slightly criminal, or take to drink, and so on. They are generally very endangered personalities because they have that low threshold and are so near to the absolute knowledge of the unconscious.

Almost all non-number divination techniques are based on some kind of chaotic pattern, which actually is exactly like the Rorschach test. One stares at a chaotic pattern and then gets a fantasy, and the complete disorder in the pattern confuses one's conscious mind. We could all be mediums, and all have absolute knowledge, if the bright light of our ego consciousness would not dim it. That is why the medium needs an *abaissement du niveau mental* and has to go into a trance, a sleep-like state, to pull up his or her knowledge. I have myself observed that in states of extreme fatigue, when I am really dangerously physically exhausted, I suddenly get absolute knowledge; I am much closer to it then, but as soon as I have slept well for a few nights then this wonderful gift is gone again. Why? Absolute knowledge is like candlelight, and if the electric light of ego consciousness is burning, then one cannot see the candlelight. If one looks at a chaotic pattern, one gets befuddled, one cannot make head nor tail of it. If one looks for a moment at a Rorschach card with its accumulation of dots, that blots out the functioning of the conscious mind, and then an unconscious fantasy comes up — "Oh, that looks like an elephant," or something like that.

So one can get information from the unconscious by looking at a pattern. Now the diviner, the sorcerer, is generally a mediumistically gifted personality and he may use tea leaves, or coffee grounds, or look into a crystal. Different lights flicker if one looks in a crystal; it has a chaotic pattern as well as an order, but the light effects are chaotic.

Primitive societies very frequently look into a bowl of water, or like the people in Uri whom I mentioned, they look at the cracks in a mud path, or any such random pattern. That blots out one's conscious thoughts. One cannot make head nor tail of a chaotic pattern; one is bewildered and that moment of bewilderment brings up the intuition from the unconscious. That is what the palmist pulled out. His confession when I squeezed him made clear to me why so many, many divination techniques all over the world use a chaotic or half-ordered pattern to get information. That, to my mind, is a primitive divination technique and it has been rediscovered, for example, in the Rorschach test.

There are many other ways of doing it. For instance, it is of great value to encourage an analysand to paint abstract or random paintings. He makes a few dots first (as in the Rorschach test) and thinks, "That looks like an elephant," and he puts a trunk on. Generally if you ask an analysand how he made his pictures he can tell you exactly how he began, with a dot, say, which looked like a rabbit, so he put a tail on, and then invented the whole picture and so an unconscious fantasy unfolds. That is one source of divination. Another is like provoking a dream in daytime. Instead of waiting

40

till one dreams in the night, one can provoke a dream in daytime by fantasying into a dot or into a chaotic pattern and so get the daytime dream. Probably we dream all the time, not only in the night but also in daytime, but because of the brightness of our conscious life we are not aware of it.

This idea is substantiated by the following fact. If one watches the mistakes in speech, or in thinking, which people make, one can observe that the dream they had the night before or the night after is generally related. Or if perhaps one wants to say "Mr. Miller" and by sheer idiocy one says "Mr. Johnson," one wonders why one made that silly mistake — one knows Miller is Miller, why did one say Johnson? That's a slip of the tongue, and generally one notices that either the night before or the night after one dreams of Johnson. He was already there. Sometimes in such a slip of the tongue one mentions someone not thought of for thirty years, and promptly one dreams of that person. Probably one already dreamt of that man in the daytime, but without being aware of it, and it only pushes itself up in a mishap, in a *lapsus linguae*.

Freud noticed this fact and pointed out that mistakes in speech and dream motifs are akin. One should go even further and say that both give the same information about something going on in the unconscious. It is therefore rather probable that a dream process continues in daytime. Looking at a chaotic pattern is like putting one's mind to sleep for a minute and getting information about what one is fantasying or dreaming about in the unconscious. Through the absolute knowledge in the unconscious one gets information about one's inner and outer situation.

Now why should that palmist, Spier, get information about *my* past, which is, so to speak, my memory possession? My past is my own and only I know it, how can he get that? I noticed that though he told the truth about my past he also told me a lot about my character. He pointed out certain things and I thought: "Oh brother, you are the same type!" Then I did a check on that and had many hand readings made for me, many horoscopes made, if possible by people I more or less knew, and I found out that they were all true. When I read them I could always say: "Yes, that's true, that is a true diagnosis." But if you were to read them, you would see that they are *most* different, and if you read them with more understanding you would see that it is typical for *that* person to notice *that* in me, and it is typical for that other person to notice

41

something else. So the information is filtered by the personality of the medium, or the diviner, or the horoscope maker, or the palmist, and so on; they get within the area of another's psychic constellation that is akin to theirs. All are true, but all are only partial.

That is my experience. I cannot make a theory of it for I have not enough comparative material, but it seems right to me that it should be so, because we know that is also true in everyday life. We can only answer to those facets of another personality when we have a certain amount ourselves. That is why there are certain people whom we cannot analyse. We have not their number, to use that expression again. We can analyse only those people whose number we have. We can contact them to a greater or lesser extent, but we can only to a certain extent understand the other. The more conscious we are, the more people we can understand, but never everybody, and the more we are conscious of the many, many inner possibilities we have, the more likely we are to be able to get the number of other people; otherwise we are one-sided analysts who can only analyse a certain type of person, or a certain type of neurosis, or other disease. There we are good specialists and can do really good work but in another field we cannot.

For instance, I cannot analyse hysterical people. I have not had an hysterical case in my practice for over twenty years, but it does not matter because they do not come to me. I have no chance to fail with them because they smell a rat, they do not come to me, and if I meet them socially I am up against a blank wall, I have no empathy. In many many other forms of madness I have full empathy, but in that one I fail and I know from talking with colleagues that it is the same with them. One has empathy only into certain human states and there are some which you miss. I still hope that I'll develop some hysterical traits one day and understand them; it is one of my great ambitions, but I have not reached that yet. I experience it as a lack but one cannot do much about it except go on till one has it.

As far as I have seen, the same thing applies with divination techniques as in my own life. Diviners always get something out of one number of my personality, but I have never had a horoscope or a hand reading of which I could say: "Now that defines me completely." One can say, "Yes, yes, that is true, I can see that, that is what I am like," but then one reads another and it is also correct. Now how is that? Then one notices that it has been just one photo-

42

graph, for it is just the same as with photographs. Photographs of people always give one moment's facet of the personality, which explains why one cannot look at photographs for a long time. If you have a photograph of a beloved person on your writing desk, you have to put it away after a while for it becomes dead. For a while it speaks and then suddenly one has the feeling that it is just a piece of dead paper and no longer that person. One would have to put up 365 different photographs of that person, one for every day of the year, to always have a fresh impression, because a photograph is like a divinatory guess of the personality and only one facet is filtered.

The same thing applies to divination not about a person but about a situation. In a primitive tribe it is much more likely to be right, because primitive societies live in a complete or all-inclusive *participation mystique.* They are like one body. If one man is starving they are all anxious. Very primitive societies and other human beings who are in great danger always share their food. Everything is shared, not because they are nobler than we are, but because they say: "Today I shot the caribou but in a fortnight it might be someone else so it is better to share the food we have."

When I bought my land in Bollingen the neighbours came to me and said: "We are a good neighbourhood because you see in such a little community we all have to help each other at some time, so we cannot afford to quarrel." That is true, you need only go there in the winter and get stuck in the snow when the neighbours have to pull your car out. You cannot afford to quarrel and you always go when one of the neighbours is in trouble. The whole group consists of about five houses. The people all hate each other, quite normally and humanly, within the normal framework. They have their shadow problems and their heritage quarrels, but they never let them come up. One cannot afford it, because we are what we call *eine Schicksalsgemeinde*, a "fate community" in nature.

In mountaineering the five people who are attached to the same rope cannot afford to quarrel. They may hate or love each other as much as they like, but beyond sympathy or antipathy it is a vital *Schicksalsgemeinde*, a fate community, and so are the primitive communities of man. They always have common troubles and problems, there are very few individual problems; therefore for the diviner of the tribe who throws the chicken bones to find out if there will be rain or good hunting, it is of as much importance to him as to all the people who stand around and watch. So there is a tremendous collective concern and with that a tremendous load of psychic energy; there is a tremendous tension, which makes it very likely, naturally, that the diviner will be inspired to get that information from the unconscious which refers to the situation, and not an answer to his personal problem.

If divining fails, one can generally see that the diviner has a personal neurotic problem which he projects into the material. Suppose my palmist had just been in great trouble with his girl friend — he might then have divined that I had love trouble and had not been faithful at that time. When there is a failure, therefore, it is generally seen to be a projection of the diviner's personal problem which blots out the other person's problem. In primitive communities there are not many personal problems; a personal problem is really everybody's problem in a fate community, so the diviner will probably not often project personal nonsense but will function correctly. From the group unconscious he extracts the answer to the group's question, and these chaotic means are the technique.

There is a higher form of oracle where numbers, or a random pattern with a certain order, are used. For instance, the oldest oracle form in China was to put fire under the shell of a tortoise and then see how it cracks; naturally it cracks along certain lines, and from that they read the fate. The pattern on the back of a tortoise is hardly a random pattern, it is relatively ordered in squares, to a certain extent like a matrix, but not quite accurately, not in exact lines — it is between order and disorder. The same applies to the crystal: the crystal has a very definite order but the light effects are chaotic and change constantly — you need only turn the crystal to get completely different light effects. If you look at a diamond you will see the same thing, for the light is in different irridescent colours, so it is an admixture of random pattern plus order.

Man first used such means in divination techniques; as far as I can see, the most primitive oracles are random patterns — Rorschach things so to speak. Later they begin to have a random pattern coordinated with a certain order, or they make a certain order — for instance, the chicken-bone oracle in certain African tribes by which one gets an inspiration, or finds an answer to whatever question one has in mind, from the way the bones thrown on the ground have fallen. Or there is a more involved technique in which one puts down a red, a black, and a white stick and then one throws the chicken bones — and with that comes a theory. Before there was no theory, but with order there comes one, that if there are more bones on the red-black band it means bad luck, and so on, so they put some kind of matrix, or one could say Cartesian coordinates, into the random patterns, either two bands or Cartesian coordinates, or they use a natural material which is a mixture of random pattern and order and then they develop a theory. Only when the order pattern is combined with a random pattern do they apply a theory, saying if this is so, then it means that, and if it is this, it means this. Before one simply looked into the water, or at the cracks in the row, and got a hunch; there was no theory that a certain crack meant something, one just got a hunch from a chaotic picture.

There are other techniques which are much, much older than any rational scientific techniques. They came to our part of the world from the 6th century before Christ and in central Asia much before then, but still, looking at the history of mankind as a whole, that would also be recent. The chaotic pattern plus order oracle I would call the real beginning of science, historically, for with it the random pattern was put into some mathematical order, either by lines, a matrix, or a system of coordinates or numbers.

Number was always used in a binary form, for the primitive mind — and we ourselves when we are in a practical situation — cannot deal with subtleties. Under the hard conditions of primitive life, questions become simple: Shall I go on that journey or not? Shall I find a bear or not? Survive or die? Does my wife deceive me or not? Will my sick child die or survive? Those are all vital questions, which in the primitive mind take on the form of a Yes or a No, and that is still how our most developed logic functions — with a Yes or a No, a plus or a minus. We have a two-positional logic and we have two positions in our mind. For instance, primitive people very often do not go into the subtlety of dream interpretation. They decide only whether it is a good or a bad dream, and that is a tendency towards the Yes or No. If they have a good dream they carry on with life, if it is a bad dream they stay in bed or in their tents and do not move about for a while. That is the simplest Yes or No problem. They always decided that way and had no developed dream theories. If a Roman senator had what he decided in the morning was a bad dream, and he did not understand it as we would, then he just stayed in bed the whole day and did not go to the Senate. There are many such stories.

Very often my analysands come in, sit down, and say, "I had a good dream," or "I had a bad dream last night." It is often not at all true, for when one analyses the dream, what they have called a bad dream is quite hopeful, and what they called a good dream is not all sugar, but they are still as primitive as that. If the general picture, and what they get from it first hand, seems good then they come in beaming: "I had a good dream!" So we are still like that and the basic problems, the vital problems of man, are still with us. We must not deceive ourselves — they are the Yes or No questions and either a matrix has been used to put order into disorder, or to give some orientation in the disorder, or numbers are used. Naturally they were first used in the Yes or No way, as we still do. We throw a coin and either get heads or tails, or we take a lot of pebbles and count them, and then get either an odd number, leaving one over, or leaving an even remainder, and then the even or odd remainder is the Yes or the No, which is the basis of the I Ching, a binary number system which answers Yes or No. Those were the first beginnings of putting a theory and a system into the random awareness that unconscious man used before.

If you think about it, that step of going from the random pattern, the Rorschach pattern, as a source of information, to the pattern which contains a geometrical or numerical order, is coincident with the possibility of forming a general theory. For instance, if there are more bones on this side then it is an unfavourable oracle, and when there are more on the other side the oracle is favourable. In detail one can read more out of that, but that is the separation of the Yes and the No. Or, if you use pebbles and the binary system, there will not only be a prediction of what is happening or information on what is going on in the unconscious, but an order has been imposed, one favourable or unfavourable for action. In certain primitive societies that is always spontaneously associated with good and bad, just as we speak naively of good dreams and bad dreams.

The Chinese had another way of looking at it, not so much separating good and bad, in the moral sense, or the lucky and unlucky, but seeing how it fitted into their great world order of Yang and Yin — the masculine and feminine principles, the active and passive, the light and the dark, and so on — having the wiser attitude that nothing is absolutely good or absolutely bad. So it would be more important in imposing a binary order to these chaotic orders not to make it good or bad — Yes or No — but to see it as such and such a type of situation, to which such and such a type of attitude fits. Yin and Yang are neither good nor bad. In China, either can be good or bad — that is another category — but when the Yin situation prevails one must behave in a Yin manner, and when the Yang situation prevails one must behave in a manner fitting that situation.

So the binary order imposed on things can either be moral, or it can be favourable or unfavourable, or it can as in China belong to this category of existence, to this rhythm of existence, which to my way of thinking is a superior attitude because it is not a personal judgement. To see everything egocentrically is very primitive. Is it good for me, is it bad for me? — that is primitive and egocentric.

The Chinese were detached and philosophical enough to say that even if it is bad for me it might be good as a whole. From the beginning they had a wiser or more objective view of what we call good and bad, and saw it more as something in the ensemble of existence. That is the beginning of science — it has the essentials of what we now call the experimental method for there is a question in the mind of the one who asks, and a mathematical method for approaching the chaos of existence and then drawing a conclusion. That is exactly what we do in the most modern physical experiment: the experimenter has a question in his mind, he has a mathematical method of approach, and then he looks at the result of the experiment and judges from the mathematical model. One might say that such types of oracle were not only the birth of theoretical science but also of experimental science; theory and experiment were not yet pulled apart but were one thing.

The simplest step was taken when the human mind began to ask the chaos of existence a question with mathematical order in it, and then awaited the result, thus giving the actual chance element a possibility. Now you see how far things have developed. What was once one thing has been pulled into two extremes. Imagine a modern physical experiment either by sight or with a bone, or whatever you like to think of, and throwing an I Ching. All have the same root; they were once the same thing, but one part has been very specifically developed and the other has remained in its archaic form. The great problem is now the interesting or exciting factor of chance.

In physical experiments chance events are a nuisance. If something goes wrong in an experiment, if by chance something unexpected happens, e.g., if there is a mathematical prediction that the result should be so and so and the result is completely different, then the scientist is in despair. Then there are two possibilities: either his calculation was wrong, in which case he changes his mathematics, or fudges his equation, as they like to do nowadays, or else he tries to find out what chance has intervened — perhaps the heat was too great or there was a flaw in the instrument. There can be fatigue and other such unfortunate things, and then they fight desperately trying to eliminate the chance event, to define and then eliminate it, to set it aside. Naturally no physical or scientific experiment nowadays is recognized as valid when done only once. One experiment means nothing to a scientist. Once an electrochemist told me that the truth of an experiment is when he makes the same experiment fifty times and always with the same result; he publishes it in a paper and a Japanese in Tokyo repeats the experiment and gets the same result, and only then is it completely valid.

So chance is the enemy — chance is what you have to eliminate by as much repetition as possible, and if the fault is in the setup or the temperature, or fatigue of the material, or so on, then you do everything possible to eliminate that in the next experiment, under conditions as similar as possible, so as always to get a similar result. Naturally chance is an objective factor and exists, but in science one speaks of a chance *accident*, something to be regretted.

Now you see the link with the calculus of probability and statistics, for they too are tools to eliminate chance. Mr. Kennedy has just told me that gambling in eliminating chance goes on wildly in insurance companies' calculations and statistics. What they really have to fight is chance, so they first eliminate suicides because that does not fit their certificate — they eliminate chance in order to arrive at the average American driver with his average security. Naturally that does not do, chance still plays tricks, and under English law, even officially in the courts, chance which is not foreseen by the insurance companies is called an act of God. That is the official term! Chance is an act of God.

When I once lectured in Geneva a physicist asked me what was the archetypal basis of chance. I was surprised by the question for at that time I had not thought about it. In primitive mentality there is no chance. What we scientifically call chance is an act of God, or of any god naturally; in a polytheistic religion it is a god or a spirit, or any magical power. There is no meaningless, accidental chance, every chance is the act of a divinity; that is the difference, but you see how far things have fallen apart. The common archetype, the archetype which we have now already named twice, is the archetype of play. If you are a gambler, and I hope you are, then you know that one is always torn between two possibilities — either to have a system, or to trust to what I would call the unconscious, and what another gambler would call his god of luck, Lady Luck, or whatever.

I remember when I was young I played bridge passionately. We did not play for money, so it was not interesting to win or lose. At first I played because it was interesting, but when you play every day, or for hours every Sunday, then you lose interest. However it never lost its interest for me because I set out to gamble with my unconscious. I did not call it that because I did not know any psychology at the time, but when the cards were distributed I shut my eyes and tried to know whether I would get good or bad cards and then I was satisfied if I had been right. Later I found out that when I sat down at the table on Sunday afternoon, I already *knew* that this afternoon I would have a run of good or bad luck. I just knew when sitting down at the table! So I was contacting what we call the absolute knowledge of the unconscious, and the fun of the game was to find out if you could really have that.

Most games played are a mixture of chance and calculation. You can use your intelligence to a certain extent but there is always the chance factor. Mah-jong, bridge, and so on, are all based on such situations. Wherever you use dice or cards there is generally a mixture. That is very satisfactory because it is an image of life which is something you can organize to a certain extent with your intelligence and reason, and if you are reasonable in life you have a better chance of a good life than if you are unreasonable, but to a certain extent there is always the act of God. So most games are in a way images of life; you can use your reason but you are up against chance and those are the most beloved and widespread types of games.

In chess it is different, because there it is absolutely a question of intelligence. If you have superior mathematical intelligence you are more likely to win than to lose, but it is very amusing for there too there is a psychological factor. I am an idiot at chess, but I am less of an idiot when I am in a rage. I played chess for a long time with my father. We played very quickly without thinking much, not professionally, for we played two games in one evening, so you can imagine that we were like children. We just sat for a minute and then made a move. I always lost the first game, even if I took a lot of trouble consciously, and I always won the second, without exception, because after having lost the first I got hot and in a rage

49

and then had the libido and enormous concentration, so I got brighter than before.

If you have a good day you get your libido into it and then your mathematical gifts function, and if it is a bad day and you are in rotten form, then you cannot concentrate. Even if you have average intelligence, it won't function, so even there there is chance and a psychological factor — the unconscious is in it as well, and that makes it so exciting. In squeezing other people who like to play I found out that, consciously or unconsciously, with most people that factor plays a role, it is really part of the fun of the game, this playing with synchronicity, playing with one's own unconscious, playing with one's own mood factors, otherwise it would really be uninteresting. If you play for money then it is simply symbolised, you either play with your unconscious libido or you represent it with money, which is a symbol of psychic energy. True gamblers do not care about the money but they want to win. Most gamblers do not really play for money; if they do, then money is a symbol for that psychic energy, that power, they play with.

Now what is the difference between a modern, physical scientific experiment and a divination oracle? In a physical experiment chance is eliminated, one pushes it out on the border as far as possible and then the little remains which cannot be eliminated. That is annoying and then one says, "Oh well, that's bad luck," but the scientist says, "We can ignore that," and that is the last condemning word. It is such a small matter that we can ignore it. In the oracle one takes a different, complementary approach, namely one takes chance as the centre; you take a coin and throw it and the very chance that it falls heads up is the source of information. So in one, chance is the source of information, and in the other chance is the disturbance or the factor one eliminates. They are absolutely what in modern scientific language one would call complementary to each other. The experiments eliminate chance, the oracle makes chance the centre; the experiment is based on repetition, the oracle is based on the one unique act. The experiment is based on a probability calculus and the oracle uses the unique, individual number as a source of information.

Now we have to ask ourselves how number can give information as to what is going on in the unconscious, and that will be the next lecture.

Lecture 3

During the last lecture I commented on the connection between the calculus of probability and oracles and other techniques of divination, and finally returned to the form of divination in which one is not confined to a random pattern into which to project one's unconscious knowledge, but where one tries to establish order by means of a matrix, for instance with a tortoise shell, or certain numbers of lines.

As I mentioned before, though the calculus of probability is only an abstraction and does not give definite information, modern scientists are firmly convinced that by it one can explore the truth about outer reality. There are, however, a certain number of more philosophically oriented physicists who have realized that the view of the world acquired by the calculus of probability is a mental artifact.

I would like to refer you to a book by Sir A. Eddington, *The Philosophy of Physical Science*, which though rather old is still valid in the main, and by which even a lay person can easily understand the practical inclusions and conclusions of modern physicists. In his book Eddington stresses a point which has caused him to be attacked by the communist camp of physics. He adheres strongly to Bohr's and Heisenberg's standpoint of quantum physics, and therefore points out emphatically that chance must be an objective factor in nature with which the scientist has to cope, and that the calculus of probability which presupposes chance is ultimately, if you reflect, a construct of the mind. What lies behind that, he says, we could just call "life" or "consciousness" or "the mind."

Let us assume that the I Ching, or a geomantic oracle, has a certain quality parallel to physical probability, since it also is an at-

51

tempt by which to explore psychological probability. Though psychological facts are in part random or individual "just-so" facts, there are also certain psychological structures or trends towards a psychological probability which one tries to clarify by means of the oracle. I will go into this in more detail later. The big difference, which I have already pointed out, between the physical experiment and the oracle is that the experiment acquires precision by repetition. The more often a physical experiment is repeated with the same result, the more accurate the result will be. No natural scientist will ever accept a statement published in a paper to the effect that such and such an experiment has been made once with such and such a result. He would reject it, saying that the experiment needs to be repeated as often as possible, so as to be certain of excluding the chance which might interfere with a particular result; if an infinite number of repetitions gives the same result then it may be taken to be accurate.

The oracle has a complementary standpoint in that it takes chance as its basis and is accurate only if thrown only once, making the chance result the centre of reflection. Therefore one might say that the experiment is repeated in time with the object of obtaining information about a little bit of reality. One cannot make an experiment without first cutting out a little area of reality within which one tries to obtain information through experiment. The oracle is exactly the opposite, for as far as time is concerned it is unique, because it is thrown only once, and the object is not to obtain information about a fraction of reality but if possible about the whole outer, inner, present, and future psychological situation. In that way it is completely complementary to the physical experiment.

The unique event which never quite fits the result of a physical experiment is nowadays called a boundary condition, or the unique results are called boundary conditions in physics. Eddington says, quite rightly, that if we could find a law which governs these boundary conditions, then we would discover another law of nature. So far this has not yet been formulated. In other words, in physics there is a whole field of facts which one calls boundary conditions, objective chance events, for which no law has yet been found.

According to Eddington, such boundary conditions always exist and with them he includes the area of reality which he calls the acts of volition of man. Man's volition, he considers (with a materialistic outlook), stems from a certain speck in his brain matter which, in contrast to other aspects of matter, can produce acts of volition and thus break through the ordinary laws of the material world — though how that functions and why has not yet been discovered. We would consider that he was still projecting the psyche onto the brain, as is usual in modern medicine, and therefore suspects that a little speck of brain matter can make acts of volition. That, he says, is the great mystery or the great question which the physicist cannot solve and then, as always, he eliminates it from the field by saying that it would not be a problem for physics anyhow.

So you see he just hands it over to another faculty. However, just *that* we would pick up as interesting, and ask what lies behind an act of volition. There we are at once in deep water, because there are actually volitions of the ego complex as well as of an unconscious complex. Even an unconscious complex can make an act of volition or decide or arrange something, as an ego can. In a way there are as many little egos as there are autonomous complexes in a human being; like the sun among the stars, the ego complex rules, but in an unanalysed personality there are these little specks around, all of which are capable of acts of volition.

Jung tried to define such acts of volition quite generally by saying that they spring from disposable energy. For instance, will-power, according to Jung, is energy which is at the free disposition of the ego complex. Thus actually the old oracle techniques were attempts to find out the probabilities or relative regularities of the psychological human situation. Almost all oracle techniques should be used like the I Ching, that is, only in very serious situations and not as a drawingroom game, as for instance when a few people sit together and say: "Let's throw an I Ching and find out something." One should only use the oracle when one has a burning question, or if one is at an impasse and in a state of emotional tension, but not when things are going smoothly and one is really not concerned with any particular problem.

We know that big inner tensions generally occur when an archetype is constellated. Someone having an archetypal dream is generally in a state of high dynamic tension, which is why Jung defines the archetypes as being the nuclear dynamisms of the psyche. Each archetype is also like a mass of dynamic energy, and in a schizo-

53

phrenic, for instance, such a load can explode the ego complex if the tension is too great. That shows empirically how high the tension of an archetype can become, for it can even destroy the whole conscious personality. In a tense situation it is extremely probable that in the unconscious an archetype is constellated; that is the moment to use the oracle because only at such a time is it likely to function and give an answer which makes sense. Thus the archetype is, in a way, a factor of psychological probability.

In other words, if there is an archetype constellated in one's analysand's or patient's unconscious, one can to a great extent predict his reactions and problems, because — if one knows how — it is possible to read such a pattern and at the same time reconstruct the conscious situation and problems, and so on. I have sometimes done that, involuntarily, without wanting to show off, for it has often happened that someone in the first hour has told me an archetypal dream as an introduction to him or herself, and then I have said: "Well then, probably consciously you are that and that, and generally in life you bump your head against these and these situations and probably you have such and such a philosophy in mind." When they have asked how I knew that, I have replied that it was not certain, but probable because of the unconscious constellation. If the unconscious is constellated in a certain way then the whole psychological situation is probably so and so. One can even reconstruct to a certain extent — not completely but in outlines — the area of the conscious problem from the unconscious constellation.

The archetype could therefore be defined as a structure which conditions certain psychological probabilities, and oracle techniques are obviously attempts to get at these structures. Jung says in his paper on synchronicity that synchronistic events — and he classifies all divinatory hit or miss techniques as experiments which have to do with synchronicity — are acts of creation and in that way they are unique. A synchronistic event is a unique, "just-so" story and not predictable precisely because it is always a creative act in time and therefore not regular.

If, for instance, an analysand has a big archetypal dream and is upset and in a tense state, it is extremely likely that synchronistic events will happen in his surroundings. Just suppose he throws an I Ching and gets 34, "The Power of the Great." It is a description of a state of great tension, in which the oracle says that the car breaks apart, and the Commentary is that the car with its four wheels, the basis of consciousness, breaks apart. That would mean that the whole conscious world of this patient would or might break down. Then he goes out after the hour and has a very bad car accident. One might then say: "Ah, the oracle even predicted that, it spoke literally about the car breaking apart — what a miracle!" But if one thinks of it more concretely, that was not really predicted. The analysand could just as easily have gone home and only dissociated consciously and not had a car accident. It is never possible to be sure from an oracle as to what will actually happen.

Synchronistic events *are* thus indisputably unique acts of creation, just-so stories, and are in themselves not predictable. But then one asks: "Why have oracles at all? Why the probabilities if one cannot predict?" Now there are psychological probabilities or, as Pauli once described them, *Erwartungskataloge*, that is, catalogues or lists of expectations, which means that the calculable probability in physics would lie between two limits. One cannot say that the next experiment will have exactly such and such a result, but it can be said that it will lie within a certain area of probability and not outside it. Therefore nowadays the calculus of probability is a list of expectations, or expected results.

One could compare that to an oracle. Suppose one gets a certain I Ching number, that is a list of expectations of psychological events, including synchronicity. If the analysand throws the "breaking of the car" hexagram, which means breaking up, or breaking apart, or the danger of the breaking apart of the conscious mental structure, it only says that if there is a synchronistic event it will belong qualitatively in that area, and not, for instance, that that afternoon he will meet his future bride. If something happens to him in the form of a synchronistic event it will be in the area of the breakdown of his conscious movements, but exactly what will happen cannot be predicted. In that way one could say that an oracle is never accurate. That is what is so irritating and what rationalists always use as an argument against oracles, for an oracle always uses a kind of general symbolic picture, which can be interpreted, like all symbols, in many forms and on many levels.

Very accurate thinkers get irritated with oracle techniques because they are so indefinite. Naturally anything can be read into them, and because it is all so vague, foolish superstitious people always see a connection and after the event say that it was in the oracle. One might say it is all so vague that practically *anything* could

55

happen, but that is just not true, that is an emotional argument born of a prejudice. It is true, however, in so far as an oracle technique is never quite accurate and cannot predict exactly. Just as a physicist cannot predict a unique event completely accurately, an oracle cannot predict a precise psychological event. But it can give an "expectation list," which can cast an image of a certain area or qualitative field of events and predict that something is going to happen within that field. There is a certain psychological probability because of what Jung calls the collective unconscious.

Since our most basic psychological structure is formed by the archetypes — which means generally collective patterns of behaviour, we all tend to react in the same way in certain situations. To give an example, suppose a primitive tribe is in a fix and cannot extricate itself by ordinary means or by dreams or common sense. They cannot cope with the situation. What is then very likely to get constellated in the unconscious is the archetype of the hero, or the saviour, for now an unusually heroic psychological effort and the mobilization of unusual superhuman "capacities of the psyche" are needed to overcome the difficulty. An individual might dream of heroic deeds or of parts of a hero myth, for instance, at such moments, when it generally happens that the hero-image is projected somewhere.

That happened when Germany projected the hero-saviour image on Hitler. That was in a time of terrific crisis, both psychologically and economically and in every respect. It came after those terrible years which preceded the Second World War, when there was so much unemployment and inflation and a complete mental and religious disorientation. In a way it was true that the only way out of this difficulty was by a tremendous change of attitude, and that mobilized the idea of a leader hero, or a saviour, in the unconscious — but it was projected onto a criminal psychopath, and that led the whole thing down the drain. Actually, in 1923 poems and literary material were written, and Germans had dreams, which show how in such unusual, difficult situations the saviour-hero archetype begins to constellate in the unconscious. Had the projection fallen on a timely, gifted, and ethical personality, he might have led the people out of the fix, but it fell on a psychopath, with all the consequences of that. That is only one example to show there is such a thing as a psychological probability in the archetypal layer of the psyche, and the possible prediction of what is coming. Divination oracles, to my mind, are attempts to contact the dynamic load of an archetypal constellation and to give a reading pattern of what it is.

As I intimated in my last lecture, behind the calculus of probability, actually and historically, lies the archetype of gambling. An oracle also can be likened to throwing dice. In the I Ching one counts yarrow stalks or throws coins for heads or tails, which is the same as throwing dice. For many oracles, instead of coins one throws dice to get a certain number and then one looks up what that means. It has to do with a chance throw, so the archetypal idea is behind both the oracle and the modern experiment. Therefore we have to go briefly into the problem of gambling and especially of playing dice.

Last lecture we discovered that the capacity to count everything, to integrate consciously the whole infinity of natural integers, was something the godhead originally had, or one could say that all the symbols of the Self have this capacity. For instance, we read in the Bhagavadgita that the god Krishna says of himself: "I am the game of dice. I am the Self seated in the Heart of Beings. I am the Beginning and the Middle and the End of all Beings. I am Vishnu the Beaming Sun among shining bodies." And in the Shatapatha-Brahmana of the Yajur-Veda, the fire god Agni says the same thing about himself. The priest throws down the dice with the words: "Hallowed by Svaha, strive ye with Surya's rays for the middlemost place among brethren! For that gaming ground is the same as ample Agni and those dice are his coals." So Agni, the fire god, is the gaming ground and the burning coals are his dice.

Jung comments on these texts, which he quotes, in "The Philosophical Tree": "Both texts relate light, sun, and fire, as well as the god, to the game of dice. Similarly the Atharva-Veda speaks of the 'brilliance that is in the chariot, in the dice, in the strength of the bull, in the wind,' " and so on.* The brilliancy corresponds to the primitive idea of *mana* and means therefore something which has an emotional or feeling value. In primitive minds the emotional intensities are the important thing and therefore are identified with all sorts of factors — with rain, storm, fire, the power of the bull, and the passion of the game of dice, because, as Jung says: "In emotional intensity, game and gambler coincide."

---

*Collected Works, Vol. 13, par. 341

It is because of the passionate, emotional intensity with which one is gripped in gambling that one becomes, so to speak, the game. Every true and decent gambler is right in it, his mind is occupied with it, he just waits and prays that the dice will fall in a certain way. That is the great pleasure in it. One lives when one gambles. One is right in it and involved, which is why primitives, for instance, even play for their wives and children, or their own heads: If I throw a six, I may behead you, and if you throw a six, then you may behead me. And they do it! They are passionate enough to put even their own heads on the gambling table. That happens again and again among North American Indians, or they gamble for their whole possessions — their wives, children, horses, everything. They come back from the gambling ground with nothing but their lives, and sometimes they go as far as to put even that at stake. If there is such a passion, then we know an archetype is at work, as illustrated by these Indians and numerous other examples.

A famous saying of the philosopher Heraclitus is that Aion (the *durée créatrice,* the eternal, creative, divine Time, which is what Aion means in Greek) is a boy who plays a board game — a boy rules the cosmos. Here again is the coincidence of the image of the god of energy, for as you know, Heraclitus thought that the world energy consisted of fire, and the ultimate control of this energy — this fire which turns into matter, into psyche, into all factors, into God, and souls, and real things, that one fire — is in the hands of a gambling boy god, a boy god who just gambles on a board game with this energy.

Again there is the connection of psychic energy and gambling. When the god — that is, the archetype of the Self, the spirit of the unconscious — gambles, he creates fate, because its creation is a synchronistic phenomenon. That is why man tried with mathematics and arithmetic and number oracles to track down the board game of the godhead. The godhead gambles with reality and man tries to track it down by these numerical methods.

Richard Wilhelm describes the functioning of the I Ching quite typically by the following picture. The relationships and the facts of the Book of Changes could be compared with the network of an electric circuit, which penetrates all things. It has the possibility of being lit up but it does not light up unless the person who puts a question has established contact with a definite situation. One should therefore not throw an I Ching without first asking: "What

58

question do I really have in mind? What do I really want to ask?" By that one makes contact with one's unconscious, and asks it to suggest what the difficulty is behind the question. "What would be the situation if one took on that new job?" Or whatever else one wants to ask. When the questioner establishes contact with the specific situation he has in mind, the network and the electric current are excited and the situation is lit up for a moment.

That is of course only a simile Wilhelm uses to illustrate what happens when you consult the I Ching, but it is typical that he thinks of it as if there were an enormous network which encompassed all possibilities. By asking the question one presses, so to speak, an electric switch, and then a certain part of the network is lit up. This naturally belongs in the whole setup of the Chinese view of the world.

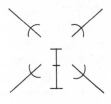

Figure 4. *Suan-shu*—to calculate, to divine.

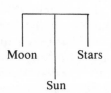

Moon | Stars

Sun

Figure 5. *Shih*—to exhibit, make manifest, proclaim.

Figure 6. *Shih*—(later writing).

In China the word for arithmetic, for calculating, has two radicals (Figure 4). In the old texts, to calculate and to divine are so close that one cannot know which is meant. One can, for instance, read texts where it says: "Master So-and-So was a great master in *Suan-shu*. He could predict the death of his friends accurately to the hour." Now we can say, "Master So-and-So was a great diviner," or "He was a great mathematician," because a mathematician was at that time an astronomer, an astrologer. All mathematical knowledge in China was used only for the purpose of divination, to such an extent that the word *Suan-shu* is used for both. The other radical of the word for calculation is one called *Shih*; that is written as in Figure 5 in the old writing, and as in Figure 6 in the later writing. *Shih* in the original meaning shows the heavens — sun, moon, and stars, those three lines — the idea being that it is the governing influence of heaven upon earthly things.

59

The old Chinese believed that heaven, the stars and the constellations of the stars, influenced situations on earth. That was summed up in the radical *Shih*, the divine influence by which the will of heaven, or Tao in Chinese philosophy, governed earthly things. This radical *Shih* is now generally translated by "to exhibit, to manifest, to make known, or to proclaim" — to make manifest, so to speak, the hidden will of the divinity, of Tao. And that was also the radical for calculation; arithmetic was nothing other, for the original Chinese mind, than a means of divining or guessing the divine will, trying to find that out by number, and that continued in China until quite recently.

The description by Richard Wilhelm of the I Ching as like a network of an electrical circuit where you light up a certain problem (Figure 7) is not a chance one. Wilhelm was so penetrated by the Chinese way of thinking that even when he used a spontaneous simile it always had a Chinese background. In my first lecture I showed you that the Chinese clearly used single natural integers or numbers in arithmetic, but that they had such number combinations as the *Lo Shou*, or the *Ho-tou*; in other words, from the very beginning they had what in modern Western mathematics is called a matrix (Figure 2, page 13). As you will remember, I explained in my first lecture the rectangular pattern in which are rows and columns up to any number. That would be a square matrix.

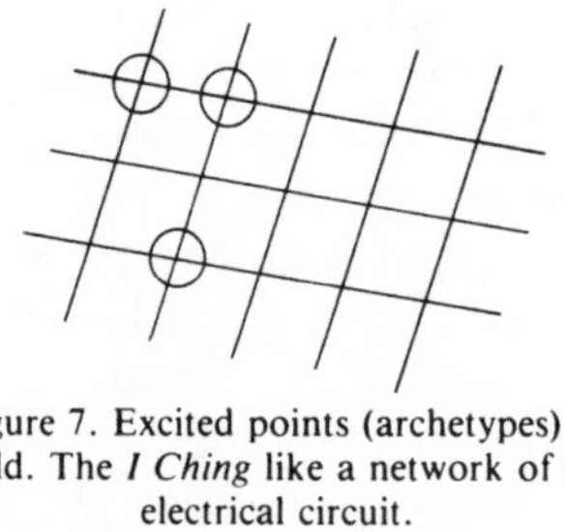

Figure 7. Excited points (archetypes) in
field. The *I Ching* like a network of an
electrical circuit.

Calculating with a whole block of numbers arranged in a certain field has only come into use in Western mathematics with the discovery by the French mathematician, Evariste Galois, of the so-called Galois field, the idea by which one mutates or permutates a group of usually four numbers. These Galois fields are used nowadays in computer and many other forms of mathematics. The idea of matrices or of such number fields, as one could call them, has more and more invaded modern mathematics. The Chinese were familiar with them but never developed them, although in some basic forms they used these matrices in their calculations from the beginning. This would correspond to the archetypal idea of the field. One could call it a field arrangement of numbers, and the concept of the field invades practically all branches of science nowadays.

For instance, in modern geometry one defines space as a manifoldness in which one can define neighbouring relations. That is the modern mathematical definition of the field, and Lancelot L. Whyte gives a general definition of the idea of field in the natural sciences when he says that it is a network of relations in every situation; i.e., in every situation there is an acting network of relations. For example, on the level of elementary particles the field consists of the tendency to take on certain ordered positions, not to move at random but to arrange themselves in a certain order. This field, as Whyte points out, is not only a conceptual framework but an active factor: an electro-dynamic field arranges the particles and actively creates order. It can naturally best be mathematically described by a matrix.

I want now to introduce a new idea, which Jung has not used, but which I think obviously lies to hand, namely that we introduce the idea or the concept of field to explore what Jung calls the collective unconscious, a field in which the archetype would be the single activated point. Wheeler, for instance, defines matter as an electro-dynamic field in which the particles are the excited points. Now I propose to use the hypothesis that the collective unconscious is a field of psychic energy, the excited points of which are the archetypes, and just as one can define neighbourhood relationships in a physical field, so one can define neighbourhood relationships in the field of the collective unconscious.

I will give an example. Let's take the archetype of the world tree — no, the Great Mother, the two are very often connected. For instance, in the tomb of the Egyptian king, Sethos the First, there is a world tree and on its trunk it has a breast from which the king drinks; he drinks literally from the breast of the world tree. The tree represents the cosmic mother who nourishes the king. Or, for instance, there are many sagas that the souls of unborn children

61

live under the leaves of the world tree and from there are carried down and born on earth, so there again the tree is a kind of maternal womb in which the earth sparks off the unborn children. Now we know that the tree is related to the sun. For instance, there are many myths where the sun is born every morning from a tree, or the sun is described as a golden apple on the tree of life. The sun is, so to speak, the fruit — it either rises from the world tree or it is the fruit of the world tree. The tree is also related to the well. In most mythologies there is a well under the world tree, a spring from which life comes.

The Great Mother is also related to the well. The well is very often a kind of maternal womb of the Great Mother and has feminine maternal qualities. The Great Mother is also related to death. For instance, on the bottom of Egyptian coffins Isis is painted, and on the cover Nut, so that the dead person actually lies in the arms of the Great Mother. Also at burial man is buried in an embryonic position, which seems to have to do with the idea that man returns like a child to the womb of mother earth, to be reborn from there.

So the Great Mother is also the Death Mother. In Roman mythology death was personified as a black woman. *Mors* is feminine in the Latin and therefore there was a female death, a kind of dark mother figure who took her children away from the earth. The tree is also connected with death because in many countries there are tree burials. Many Eskimo and many Northern tribes, like the Tunguses or Tschuks, hang the coffins of the dead on trees and thus give them back to the mother. In that case the tree, not the earth, is the mother into which the coffin goes. Also the very fact that most coffins were made from a big tree trunk made it symbolic, for the tree was also the mother who enfolds the dead person and gives rebirth.

Death is also connected with the well. There are many sagas where someone jumps into a well and thus into the world of the dead; it is the entrance to the underworld. The springs of a well sometimes rise up from the land of the dead.

The tree trunk sometimes stands for the phallus, so the tree is not only the Great Mother but the opposite, the father. For instance, at the birth of certain Aztec tribes the first year is a broken tree trunk, and they say that from it they all sprang. There the tree trunk represents a father figure, as a phallus; and you may have seen mediaeval pictures which illustrate the dream of Abraham, in which he lies in bed and from his erect penis grows a tree, and all the branches of the tree are the different ancestors of Christ. He dreamt that from him would come all those generations and eventually the Saviour. Here again the tree is a phallus and an emblem of paternity. The phallus is also connected with the sun, as you know. The Great Mother also often has to do with phallic symbols. For instance, witches have either a broom or an enormous nose with which they scratch in the oven, and so on.

If one knows enough mythology one can make a completely consistent web from every great archetype to every other great archetype. There is always a legend or a saga which links up two archetypes in a new form, and it is a tragedy people do not realize that. Writers on mythology always choose one beloved theme, let us say the sun, and then they chase through all the myths and say that everything is solar. Afterwards comes another chap who says that everything is lunar, while Mannhardt says that everything is the vegetation god, who got hung up on the tree. For Erich Neumann everything was the uroboric mother, and so on. The Chinese would say that if you pull one grass root you always get the whole meadow, and that is what Jung calls the contamination of the archetypal images.

All archetypes are contaminated with each other. Therefore to apply the idea of the field to the collective unconscious is, I think, quite justifiable and then you can say, as I said before, that the unconscious is a field in which the excited points are the archetypes and in which one can define neighbourhood relationships (Figure 8). As the mathematicians say of space, one can establish neighbourhood relationships to all other points of the field. I have pick-

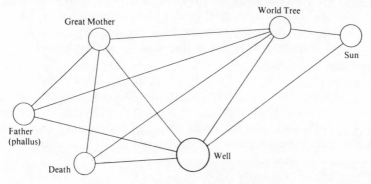

Figure 8. A field of related archetypes.

ed this archetype of the Great Mother completely at random, but as you see I could just as easily have taken the archetype of the sun and made a field around that or anywhere else, and reordered the whole thing; that is completely arbitrary.

The great question is whether the field of the collective unconscious is such an arbitrary random pattern of archetypes, a field in which the excited points are archetypes — or does it have some order? Jung has already pointed out that among the different archetypes, there is one which encompasses and regulates all the others and that is the archetype of the Self. So one should not look at the field really in that way, one should construct — though I have not yet been able to do that properly — such a mathematically ordered field and always put the archetype of the Self in the centre. It is the most powerful archetype, the one which arranges or regulates the relationships of all the others. Let us say it is an active ordering centre which regulates the relationships of all other archetypes and gives to the field of the collective unconscious a definite mathematical order. Jung constructs it from quite another angle in his book *Aion*, where he shows that the best possible mathematical model of the archetype of the Self is four double pyramids put in a ring.*

If you take four such things, make a chain of them and put them in a ring, you get that model of the Self which Jung tried to delineate from certain mythological material. The interesting thing is that if you stretch on a line the rhythm of the *Ho-tou* (Figure 3, page 13) and count along, 1, 2, 3, 4, 5 to the middle, 6, 7, 8, 9, 10 to the middle, and so on, you always return with the line to the same centre. If you now stretch the centre out to 0, 5, 10, then you get the double pyramid: 0, 1, 2, 3, 4, 5 — 5, 6, 7, 8, 9, 10 (Figure 9). You need only stretch the *Ho-tou* rhythm into a line and then you get the mathematical model Jung constructed in *Aion*. The Chinese *Ho-tou* really mirrors the same rhythm which Jung discovered in quite a different connection to be the rhythm of the archetype of the Self.

That is not surprising. If one looks at the arithmetic and mathematics of most divination techniques, they all contain that rhythm in some variation. One could call it *the* number rhythm of the Self, which is the basis of the mathematics of all divination techniques. For instance, geomancy has the same number rhythm as the I

---

*Collected Works, Vol. 9, II, pars. 390 ff.

Ching, only in reversed order. The dynamic processes in geomancy are represented by four and the result by a triad; and in China the dynamic processes are represented by groups of threes and the result is represented by a quaternio. There are the same number rhythms only in reverse, which probably has to do with the different mentality. The triads always point to dynamism and therefore to action in a situation, while the quaternios always point to, or describe, the whole situation.

The Chinese are not interested in what they should do; their interest is rather in the whole situation so that they then can act in awareness of it. Western man says he will act anyhow, but what is his situation? He does not doubt that he will act because his temperament is extraverted. So his interest is in what the situation will lead to or fits into. The Chinese are the other way round; they live in the idea of the wholeness, and action is what happens. But both have the same number rhythms, which can always be connected with the number rhythm of the *Ho-tou*, the number rhythm of this construction by Jung being the rhythm of the Self.

So we can now go on with our definition and say the collective unconscious is a field of psychic energy, the excited points of which are the archetypes, and that field has an ordered aspect which is dominated by the number rhythms of the Self, which as you will see are triads and quaternios. With the number oracles and divination techniques one tries to define the process of the Self archetype. In the ring of the four double pyramids, Jung points out that the Self is in an eternal process of constant rejuvenation. He

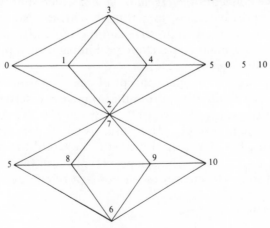

Figure 9.

65

compares it to the carbon-nitrogen cycle of the sun, where certain particles are split off and others attracted, giving finally a rejuvenated atom of the same form. It is as though the atom split off particles and attracted others, thus restoring its own form in constant self-renewal.

As far as we can observe the archetype of the Self, we can say the same thing, for it too is not static but is in a constant process of self-renewal in a certain rhythm. Because this is the dominating order or field of the collective unconscious, one could say that divination techniques are attempts, by a chance throw of numbers, to find out what is the rhythm of the Self at a particular moment. Jung sometimes describes what we do when we consult the I Ching oracle by saying that it is like looking at the world situation watch to find the moment one is in, while the oracle would give the inner and outer world situation by which to govern one's actions.

With this I still should explain — I have simply assumed it — why or for what reason the inventors of divination techniques used the whole natural integers to try to find out about the pulsations, the rhythms of the Self. We have therefore to go deeper into the problem of energy, or ask how number relates to energy, since numbers are always used to define the energic situation in the collective unconscious. Why were they used and not some other means? Why natural integers?

In order to find out, we have first to go back to the idea of energy in general. As Jung points out at the end of "On the Nature of the Psyche," the concept of energy is originally derived from the primitive concept of *energeia* or *mana*, which simply means the extreme impressiveness of something.* Whenever something is enormously or intensely impressive and therefore affects one psychologically, i.e., makes a psychological impact, then primitives say it is *mana*, or *mungu*.

Therefore the original concept of energy was more the idea of psychological intensity. From that was slowly derived the physical concept of energy. The word "energy" as used by Aristotle, or for instance the philosopher Heraclitus, is still full of mythological associations. For Heraclitus it was still the world fire pulsating according to certain rhythms, a psycho-physical factor. Later the modern scientific creator of the concept of energy, Robert Mayer,

---

*Collected Works, Vol. 8, par. 441

fell back on this old *mungu* or *mana* concept, but then redefined it in a form which could be used in science, and nowadays it has become a completely abstract concept in physics which has a value only in so far as it can be measured quantitatively.

The physicist Eddington, for instance, says energy has nowadays replaced the concept of substance in physics; it is what can be measured quantitatively and described by the calculus of probability, or at least defined quantitatively with the calculus of probability. All other aspects of the original psycho-physical concept have been eliminated. This other aspect Jung has picked up and has created the idea of psychic energy. We can look at psychological processes as being energic processes which even follow certain laws. For instance, we conceive that an individual is a relatively closed system, so there is conservation of energy. Therefore, if someone lacks energy in consciousness we assume it to be somewhere in the unconscious, and vice versa. We reckon with a certain conservation of energy, that the amount of psychic energy at the disposition of an individual is more or less the same, and therefore if it disappears in one form it reappears in another, an idea which has proved exceedingly fruitful.

Jung, however, points out that psychic energy cannot be measured quantitatively; we can still only measure it with our feeling impressions. Let us assume that an analysand comes into the room and tells a story in a completely quiet voice, having enough self-control to dominate his emotions. Easterners can tell the most horrible thing with a completely impassive smile, and a completely unaltered voice, but all the same, if you are sensitive, you feel an awful impact, as though something had hit you.

People sometimes have a terribly negative projection and hatred, and decide that they have to tell the analyst about it and have learned that that should be done decently. So they begin by saying: "Dr. von Franz, today I have to tell you what a resistance I have. I hope you will not be hurt. I know that it is really a projection but I feel I want to talk to you about it and not just stew in it." It can be most touching and completely reasonable and psychological. They will say what they have against you, and sometimes the impact is not strong but other times I feel a physical shock. If the analysand shouts and insults me, it is natural to feel shocked but one feels it even if the energy is completely held back. One feels it as an intensity of some kind. I can only use a simile and say it is

67

like being hit by something. Have you ever seen somebody looking
at you with hatred? You may, for instance, look up innocently at
a crowd of people, and somebody is staring at you and you feel as
if you had been hit physically and negatively. The same thing can
naturally also occur positively, but one is more aware of it when it
is negative. In the positive aspect it is more like an attraction.

In lecturing I notice sometimes that unconsciously I am beginning to lecture to one face in the room; my energy flows again and
again to that one person and a kind of current establishes itself.
One has not necessarily any special sympathy for that person, but
there are such attractions. Apparently one tends to turn to a person who is very passionately interested; one feels as if one were
specially listened to and one naturally turns in that direction. As
far as I can make out, it is more the intensity of the listener than
one's own liking or sympathy. That is only to illustrate our feeling
awareness of psychic intensity. We feel it but have no physical apparatus with which to show it.

Many people meet that with the objection that we have the galvanometer in the association experiment, by which one can immed-
iately see and measure psychic intensity, but that is not strictly
true if you think about it, because in an association experiment
made with the galvanometer one does not measure the psychic intensity but only the intensity of the physiological reaction. One
still moves within the physical realm, for one measures a physical
factor by physical means — that is, the physiological reaction
caused by the psychic intensity — and that gives absolutely satisfactory information, since the physiological reaction is equivalent
to the psychic intensity. We can, therefore, quite legitimately as-
sess the psychic intensity from the physiological reaction, but we
are not really measuring a psychological factor. In other words, so
far it has not been possible to measure psychic intensity, due, I
think, to our use of numbers.

In measuring we use numbers of some kind, and by them we define physical intensity. Number measures quantity, or number is a
quantity; for instance, the number five indicates that there are five
apples here. For us that is an absolutely ingrained self-evident fact.
If we go back to the origin of the use of number, we see that this
is a completely one-sided development. Self-evidently and naturally
number indicates a quantity — but in its original form it also indi-
cated the quality or the pattern of a structure, and not a quantity;

that aspect has been lost and slowly left behind in the development of number theory in the West, until in modern mathematics number is only a quantity. Therefore, naturally, if we use a quantitative number to measure physical quantities we cannot use it to measure psychic energy, because psychic energy in its essence expresses itself in quality. It is a qualitative factor, which is why Jung says we can only measure psychological intensity with the feeling function.

The feeling function, in contrast to the thinking function, informs us about the quality of things, it tells us if a thing is agreeable or disagreeable, dangerous or not dangerous, threatening or not threatening. We express qualities in adjectives. People who use many adjectives colour what they say with their feeling, whereas thinking types use very few adjectives and many nouns in their speech. The latter are only interested in the definition of what is what and ignore the quality. Artists always use many adjectives, words which express quality. If, for instance, as I described before, one feels that one is being stared at with intense hatred, one is aware with one's feeling not only that something strong is constellated, but even whether it is hostile or benevolent. One has no rational means of explaining that. If accused of being completely crazy and inventing things, one cannot give a rational explanation since it is an experience of the feeling function.

Naturally, with feeling, as with all the other functions, one can deceive oneself and make mistakes in such situations. One can assume hostility where there is none, or wrongly assume something to be of enormous importance when it really is not; the importance may lie somewhere else. So the feeling function cannot be relied upon as a certainty; like all functions it is an organ of awareness which can sometimes deceive us, but it is the only way by which we can orient ourselves in the world of quality.

Now look at what happened at the other end of the globe, namely in China. There, number developed just as one-sidedly, but it serves to describe quality and not quantity. Naturally a Chinese carpenter or mason will also measure his wall but the Chinese think that that is the lowest aspect of number; it is what artisans use, but that is the completely trivial and uninteresting aspect of number. What is interesting is that number mirrors the quality of a situation, or an ensemble, as Granet defines it.

We must now also return to the synchronistic outlook of the Chinese. In my first lecture I said that the Chinese do not ask what caused something to happen, they do not have a linear idea of time — you remember my linear scheme. We say, for instance, the barn burnt down because children played in it; the children played in the barn with matches because their mother had chased them out of the house in a bad mood, because Papa had hit Mama over the head; so the reason why the barn burnt down was father's hitting mother over the head! That is the A, B, C, D effect, the method of a police enquiry. That is the way we look at things: we always try to find out why something happened, we go back to the cause. We end with the effect and go back and reconstruct the sequence or line of events. That is causality, which till the end of the 19th century was regarded as a law, though now we know that it exists only as a probability. The Chinese ask: "What likes to happen together?" Then they explore such bunches of inner and outer events. Figure 1 (page 8) illustrates this attitude — separate events grouped around a certain moment in time.

We have a certain awareness of that too. In German we have the saying: *"Ein Unglück kommt nie allein"* — accidents never happen singly, there is always a second and a third. There is a tendency to a chain reaction. Or we say: *"Alle guten Dinge sind drei"* — all good things go in threes. There are also a lot of superstitions: if someone has two accidents then people say let's have the third and get it over, because they feel there will be a third before the bad sequence stops.

So whereas we have only a kind of superstitious popular awareness of the fact that there is a tendency of certain events to cluster together, the Chinese concentrate their whole scientific attention on just that. If you read Chinese historical chronicles, they simply say in the Year of the Dragon so-and-so the empress went off with her lover, the Tartars overran the country, the crops failed, and in the city of Shanghai there was an outbreak of the plague. Then in the next year, in the Year of the Tiger so-and-so the empress came back repentant and in that same year a dragon came out of the Tungting lake and had to be banished, or exorcized, and then certain other political events took place. That is how they wrote history and to them it was not just what we would call a random collection of facts.

Naturally Western historians despised this way of writing, because they did not understand it. They said it was just ridiculous to collect a few random facts and put them together, it was idiotic.

70

But for a Chinese reader it is completely different. He would say: "Ah-ha, that is how it all happened." For him that is complete information on the Year of the Dragon so-and-so; he has an intuitive picture of how time was constellated at that moment, and that all these things *had* to happen together.

Westerners are slowly realizing that in fact there *is* a tendency for things to happen together; it is not just fantasy, there is a noticeable tendency of events to cluster. So far as we can see, that has to do with the archetypes; namely, if a certain archetype is constellated in the collective unconscious then certain events tend to happen together.

In our history only one example of such things has been noted – the fact that when a scientist makes a new discovery, or when a big invention is made which really changes the situation of mankind, there is a tendency for several scientists at the same time and in the same year to have the same idea quite independently. Or an invention is made in the same year by two men who know nothing about each other. Then there follows a dispute about plagiarism and whether they *did* know about each other, and if one did not steal from the other; but in many such situations it can really be proved that there was no connection. The two just found the same thing at the same time. That is the Chinese way of looking at it and this is the only area in which it has been recognized by the Western mind. In honest histories of science one may find such an observation, namely that strangely enough there is a tendency for certain ideas and inventions to crop up in different places at the same time.

From a psychological point of view that is not such a miraculous thing. In the spirit of time, so to speak, certain questions and psychological problems are constellated. Then several intelligent people have the same question in mind, chase along the same alley and come to the same results, and that is due to the constellation of an archetype in the collective unconscious. I tried, for instance, in my first lecture, to tell you which archetype I think is now constellated in the collective unconscious, namely the archetype of the complete man, the Anthropos. Many events of our time, which one reads of in the papers, can be explained by showing that they all point to the same factor, that this archetype is now constellated, and crops up in a thousand forms.

The Chinese have an intuitive awareness of this, and therefore thought that the best way to write history was to obtain a real pic-

71

ture of a time moment in the past by collecting all these coinciding events, which together give a readable picture of the archetypal situation existing at that time, and that again gives the idea of a field. The events, one could say, are shown in an ordered time field, and that is the way in which the Chinese use number. Number gives information about the time-bound ensemble of events. In each moment there is another ensemble, and number gives information as to the qualitative structure of the time-bound clusters of events. That sounds complicated but it is the simplest way I can put it. If we are fair I think we have to see that number is an archetypal representation or idea which contains a quantitative and a qualitative aspect.

Therefore, before we can touch the whole problem of divination, we have to revise our view of number and of mathematics. From there we can probably approach certain other factors, which until now we could only confess we could not measure but could only approach with the feeling function.

Actually number gave information about feeling and ethics in China. Drop for a moment your prejudice that there are deeds that are good or bad in themselves — which actually is complete nonsense, for they do not exist — and say that an ethical action always depends on who does what in what moment. Of course that could be disputed! For instance, let us take murder — you could say that murder really is always a crime, but I would say: "Excuse me, what about William Tell? And what about a man who had shot Hitler in 1935? Wouldn't you have called him the most ethical person and the greatest hero in history? Even murder depends on who does what, at what moment, in what measure, and to what extent." But your feeling would revolt and say: "No, that does not come under the category of murder, that is something different." But it does come under the category of murder, for one man has killed another.

So you see that there is no objective good and evil; your feeling functions differently, depending on who does what and in what context. There the idea of measure enters. An analyst knows that. If one has to tell an analysand about a certain disagreeable shadow thing, the intensity with which one does it will depend on the circumstances. If one is a bit too intense, the other's obstinate resistance will be aroused and the whole thing will block; and if one does it too kindly, exerting no pressure, the other may listen and say, "Yes, yes," but forget all about it, it has made no impression. One has to measure what is required, and whether one does it rightly or wrongly depends on the exact emotional intensity. With too much emotional intensity the other blocks, and if it is said too kindly it goes in one ear and out the other.

Jung, for instance, said that crazy people needed electric shocks but that he would never give them with a machine; he would give them himself by shouting, or hitting the person over the head, because then he could measure them with his feeling. Then one can measure exactly how big or how small a shock is required to wake that person up. Sometimes when people are in a state of emotional possession, the only way to prevent them from snapping is by hitting them, either verbally or physically, but it all depends on the measure and that requires the feeling function. It is only by your feeling that you can tell how much your voice must be raised or whether, perhaps with a sensitive person, you may only whisper the terrible thing and then sort of appease at once and say, "Well, naturally that is not so important, everybody feels bad," and so on. Even then the other gets pale and is completely shocked. All that lies within the area of feeling — the feeling function gives the information and the measure.

There feeling has to do with measure, so why should it not also have to do with number?

Lecture 4

Last time I introduced the idea that we could conceive of the collective unconscious as a field, the excited points of which would be the archetypes. I tried to show that the network of relationships among the many archetypes is like a field in which the connections are the meaning — the field in which one can state or observe meaningful connections. Then came the question whether the distribution of the archetypes in this field was random or ordered. I ended by outlining the idea that the archetype of the Self and its arithmetical order regulates the whole field; it is a superordinate archetype regulating the distribution of the field.

That the archetypes could be seen as ordered in a field is a very old idea. Already Plato tried to construct a field in the form of a pyramid (Figure 10). He probably had in mind the Pythagorean *tetractys,* where the idea of the good would be of the highest order — in Plato's philosophy that is the image of God or of the Self, to which he subordinates all other archetypes.

Jung mentions in his paper on synchronicity a different pattern. Various attempts have been made in the past to coordinate to the archetypes certain numbers in a certain order, and so to establish a number-oriented field. Jung mentions Aegidius de Vadis, Agrippa von Nettesheim, and some others. For instance, Aegidius de Vadis says that all elements (what we would call archetypal images) are connected with certain numbers. In the whole of antiquity and very much again in the time of the Renaissance, there were numerous attempts to construct such fields, but I do not want to go into that. I only mention it to show that this idea has always roamed around in the minds of people, who had a kind of hunch that there should be such a general orderedness of the archetypes.

Now, however, in spite of this fact, we have to ask what the difference is between the archetypes of number, of numerical representations, and those of image representation. If, for instance, we take the number two as an archetypal idea or representation, it is much more abstract than the archetype of the hero, or the archetype of the Great Mother. So on one hand we have a mythological image, and on the other something abstract, namely number. In the past people simply said the god-image was one, the god-mother number two, and so on; they simply ascribed certain numbers to certain archetypes. There are infinite variations of those patterns. One could not, by looking at all those past patterns, construct any order at all. Like the myths, there are national and cultural variations and one cannot deduce an absolute order, therefore we have to ask ourselves what the difference between number and archetypal image is. If I say, for instance, "the archetype of the number two," the emphasis is on the orderedness, while if I say "the archetype of the god-image," then the emphasis is on a complex psychological feeling experience, and not specially on the order aspect of it. Therefore one could say that numbers specially emphasize the order aspect of archetypes.

There is, moreover, one mythological system, the system of the Mayas, which connects number so closely with archetypal representations that it is even contained in the names. For instance, the great hero of the Book of Counsel is called Hunabku — the name

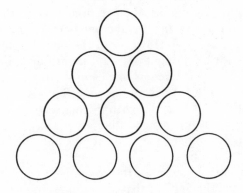

Figure 10. Aristotelian field —
archetypal picture of the Self.

75

comes from Hun, the one. There is another hero called Seven Hunter. Then there are the "eight gods," and in each of their names a number has been included. In this Maya idea one comes back to the origin of the idea, namely the time sequence, because to every godhead of that religion is allotted one day of the calendar year. The number therefore has to do with the time lapse, and I think that is the essential connection — that if we look at archetypes, or archetypal representations in which time sequences appear, there is a certain lawfulness or order. Thus numbers, when they are identified with certain mythological representations. are what one could call time numbers, for they characterize a certain moment in time.

The same is true for the mandala. In my last lecture I tried to show that the archetype of the Self and its mathematical structures represent the basic order of such fields of mythological representations. We know that the archetype of the Self very often appears in a mathematical or numerical structure, namely the mandala, which is one of its most widespread representations. Jung says that the mandala symbolizes through its centre the ultimate oneness of all archetypes. You will remember I said before that everything is everything, that one can always connect all archetypes. There is therefore always this secret oneness. In Jungian terminology they are all contaminated and are also ultimately one; the mandala through its centre symbolizes this ultimate oneness as well as the manifoldness of the world of appearance.

This is therefore an empirical correspondence to the metaphysical idea of the *unus mundus*. I will come back to this expression later, just keep it in mind. However, if the one manifests in many forms, it must not be thought of as a discontinuity, because if all archetypes are always a oneness one cannot cut that into bits, or one can arbitrarily, but it has no meaning. To observe their oneness it is better to think of a crystal with its many facets. If the crystal is rotated or its position changed, then one always sees another facet; thus seemingly we perceive many things but they are actually different aspects of one crystal.

We can therefore conceive of the collective unconscious as being ultimately always the Self, or that same one thing which transcends our grasp. So if, for instance, we dream about the single archetype of the hero or sun-god, it is as if we saw one facet, and when it rotates we see yet another facet of the very same thing. Looked at

76

from that angle *time* comes in, for which facet does one see first? There is a time sequence in what one perceives, as evidenced in mythological tales which have not only typical figures. For instance, in fairytales there is not only the typical figure of the king, or of the dummling, or of the witch, or the helpful animal, but these elements recur again and again in different forms in different myths.

An extensive survey of many mythological systems shows that certain basic elements are always retained: the divine child, the hero, the snake, the dragon, the hero's enemy, etc. These are not, however, only typical images, as we call them, but also typical sequences and connections, namely where the pearl is, there is always the dragon, and where the dragon is there is always a pearl. Or one can predict that if a hero is in connection with a helpful animal he will always succeed. In all the myths and fairytales I have studied, I have never seen a case where a hero with helpful animals does not win out. If he picks up a helpful or a grateful animal who has promised to help, with absolute certainty it can be predicted that there will not be a tragedy but a happy end. In that way one can predict the time sequence in the fairytale, and predict what will happen with a certain accuracy. This means that there are not only typical motifs but also typical sequences of archetypal events.

The physicist Wolfgang Pauli even thought that that might afford an explanation for the phenomenon of precognition — namely that we in our psyche unconsciously know which archetype is now constellated and by that can predict what will come next. In other words, the phenomenon of psychic precognition is based on this time order of the archetype.

It is interesting in this connection to see that the verb "to tell" in German is *erzählen*, which is derived from the word *Zahl*, number. *Erzählen* is "to number" an archetypal image. In French, "to tell" is *raconter*, which is akin to *compter*, to count, to enumerate, and, as Nora Mindell has pointed out to me, in Chinese the word for enumerate means *Suan*, to count the *chi*, i.e., the origin, of *lai*, which means: of what will happen, to count the origin of what is going to happen.

In these etymological structures one sees that man must originally have known that when he tells a mythological or archetypal tale, it is like counting. It follows a certain ordered rhythm of events. Those of you who have heard my fairytale lectures know that many years ago, and long before I thought about these things, I discovered that it was very useful to count the figures of a fairytale and then simply to make a scheme of what happened in the form of numbers.

I will just remind you of one fairytale to show you what I have in mind. There is a Russian fairytale called "The Virgin Czar," in which a reigning czar has three sons. Two are normal, and the third is the despised dummling who sits by the stove and scratches himself and nobody takes him seriously. It is the usual thing: what is missing is the feminine archetype. There is a quaternio, completeness, the totality, but without a female. In the ruling conscious attitude the feminine element is lacking. There is a religious idea which completely expresses the totality in its male aspect, but does not express the accompanying female aspect, so we can easily guess that the story will be about finding or incorporating the female.

The three sons go into the Kingdom Under the Sun to find the traces of where their father had been, and also probably from where he had fetched their mother who is now dead. Two sons go wrong and fail, as is usual. The third son, however, comes to three witches who are all called Baba Yaga, *the* great classical witch in all Russian fairytales, a kind of devouring Great Mother figure. These three Baba Yagas are all sisters, three aspects of the same thing, and they have a niece who is not a witch but a beautiful lady called Maria with the Golden Plait. You can guess the rest: the son comes to those witches, who send him on to Maria, and after long tragedies, which I am not going into and which are enumerated in detail, he marries Maria (Figure 11). Then he goes into another kingdom with her and Maria has twins.

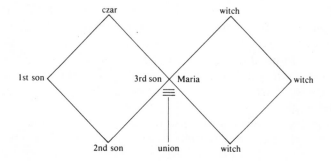

Figure 11.

78

Now you see the mathematics of the story: there is a purely masculine quaternio in collective consciousness and a purely feminine quaternio in the collective unconscious. A dynamic process, which is the "counting" of the story, ends up with three males and a female; it is still predominantly male but there is one woman, so it is a symbol of totality in which the feminine is now represented. Also the twins are little children, which means a form of renewal; so the quaternio is renewed, it has again a future and the feminine element is in it. The czar's first two sons, the brothers, are condemned to death, so what also remains is an old quaternio of the czar and the three witches, and a new quaternio, which is the real result of the story, consisting of Ivan (the third son), Maria, and her two children (Figure 12). There the future goes on, and the flow of psychic energy continues.

There is a very definite time and number sequence in all archetypal tales. It is not always, though very frequently, a play of quaternios, but there are usually triads and quaternios in fairytales which "dance" and one can in that way see that there is an absolutely mathematical structure. For instance, I have never found a single fairytale which began, "A king had three sons . . .", where the problem was not to integrate the feminine. So one can have the precognition, without knowing the story, that somehow it will take that course; one can predict the time sequence, and even to a certain extent in what way the play of the archetypes determines which next facet of the great crystal will come up and in what way it will rotate. Because people originally knew that, apparently, we

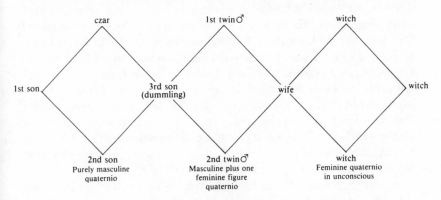

Figure 12. Infinite sequence of rhythm.

79

find in many languages the connection between "telling" a story and the idea of *Zahl*, number. This brings in the problem of energy and of time and I want now to go into that.

In the story there is an energic process: a quaternio has come to an end, has got stuck, and then there comes the flow of energy, namely the quest of the third son which brings about the desired result, the new quaternio, and then the story breaks off. All fairytales and all myths break off at a certain point but it is never a final one; it is like an eternal melody, or for instance a musical potpourri, where there is a melody and then a suspense note, and then another melody. That is what tales are like, they always end up with a slight suspense, a slight question mark. In "The Virgin Czar," for instance, I would say those two are very young and there is only one woman instead of two men and two women; it is not quite a balanced end result, but it is an improvement on the previous situation. So one can easily imagine a story where there are a king and a queen with two children who are stolen by a dragon, and so on. There are such stories which continue until they come to another result.

That is not just my arbitrary idea but that is how, for instance, the authentic storytellers work. Oriental fairytale tellers sit at the market place and simply go on the whole day; people listen for a while and then pay a bakshish and leave, but the storyteller just continues, and people who have nothing to do — and in the Orient most are like that — sit and listen the whole day long and then they have to pay a bit more. And what does the Oriental fairytale teller do? He always takes this note of suspense and just starts another story from there. He makes another chain of events and we can see that because we have these fairytales. For instance, in European collections fairytales are relatively short compared with Oriental fairytales, in a volume of oriental tales, what in European fairytales would be three or four stories, have just been joined together absolutely accurately. There is no split in the stories, they have such a feeling relationship to the archetypal connections that they always know which fairytale would be the continuation of the last and then just start the new melody, which makes those long, long chains of tales which in our countries exist as single stories.

It can therefore be said that "to tell" is to go through time in a rhythm — to go on, and on, and on, in the rhythm of the archetypes, and that this has a secret order. One cannot begin with just *any* story; one cannot, for instance, tack Snow White, or Little Red

Riding Hood, onto our story, but one could attach a story of a queen who has twins and a witch who slanders her and tells her husband, who is away at the war, that she has given birth to dogs, etc. One can only continue in a certain way when a result has been reached and not in another way, and that very fact confirms the secret order in the sequence of the archetypes. They cannot be chained together arbitrarily but in an infinite sequence of such rhythms. An archetypal tale, like a dream, represents a self-representation of the flow of psychic energy.

You know that Jung, who introduced the concept of psychic energy, also looked, in the same connection, at dreams as a flow of events, a sequence of images which represent or visualize a certain flow of energy. That is why in looking at dreams, the lysis, or catastrophe, in which they all generally end, is so important, because that shows where the flow of energy is aiming. In analysis, while I listen to a dream, I always think "and then, and then, and then?" and I keep the end sentence of a dream in mind. Sometimes people let that peter out, and I say: "Is that really the end sentence of the dream?" "Yes, there I woke up" — and then I know that that is as far as the flow of psychic energy went. We know then where the lifestream underneath consciousness is flowing and what it is aiming at, the direction in which it is going. The opening sentence of the dream is important because it shows the present situation, it shows where the dreamer is now in this world of confusion. Then come a sequence of events, and the end sentence gives the direction in which energy is flowing.

We look at dreams, therefore, as an energic process, as a visualization of the flow of the energy of the unconscious, and the same is true for mythological dreams, for fairytales and myths — the archetypal forms of this manifestation. One can always look at them from an energic standpoint. Therefore at the end of my last lecture I spoke of the problem of the relationship of physical and psychic energy, and pointed out that while physical energy can be measured quantitatively, we have no means as yet to measure the quantity of psychic energy, except by a feeling awareness of intensity. I ended my last lecture in speaking of this feeling of awareness which one has, so that even though somebody may speak of something quite quietly, one yet feels a terrific amount of energy behind what is being said; it is the feeling function which gives us this orientation.

I have been asked why I call psychic energy a qualitative pheno-

81

menon, and physical energy a quantitative one. I have done that in a very one-sided way. I have overstressed these opposites simply to get into your minds the two opposites of quality and quantity. In general we speak of the psyche as being the world of quality, for physical energy does not manifest in images, we can only understand it quantitatively. Psychic energy, on the other hand, or a psychic constellation or situation, manifests in symbols which we can only describe qualitatively. So we generally speak of the world of the psyche, and psychic energy, as a qualitative phenomenon, and of the world of physical energy as a quantitative phenomenon.

However, as Jung points out in "On the Nature of the Psyche," it is likely that psychic energy and physical energy are simply different forms of one and the same thing; therefore energy that manifests qualitatively has in fact a latent quantitative aspect, and vice versa. Modern physicists say that a quantum jump, or, for instance, the jump of one electron in its frequency to an outer orbit, changes the structure of an atom not only quantitatively but also qualitatively and therefore one cannot really separate quantity and quality, they are simply complementary mental concepts. I mean that they do not exist objectively; we can look at the same things quantitatively and qualitatively, and even physical energy has, as Viktor Weisskopf points out, a qualitative aspect, in so far as it conditions different structures. A change in quantity makes a change of structure, and thereby a change of what we would call quality.

So one can say that even physical energy, which we usually measure quantitatively, and look at from the quantitative standpoint, has a latent qualitative aspect; but it is also true that psychic energy, which we can observe mainly in its qualitative manifestation — for instance as image and so on — has a latent quantitative aspect, which consists in this impact of greater or lesser intensity. The very fact that we say this is more or less impressive, and shows it to be a quantitative and not only a qualitative statement.

Now our Western prejudice is that number can only count or express quantities; it is for us the instrument to count *quanta*. We all think of one apple, two apples — that's the quantity of apples or potatoes, or so on. But if number, according to Jung's hypothesis, is the archetype which unites the world of the psyche and matter, then it must also share something with the world of quality, and here to me it was revealing to discover that in China number is used completely qualitatively.

If you read Marcel Granet's *La Pensée Chinoise* you will find that for the Chinese number represents qualitative structures. For instance, if something is one, then it points to the whole, the universe and its lawfulness, for example, the Tao. If something is two, it points to observable reality in all domains: in music, feeling, physics, everywhere, so to speak. In other words, number conveys to the Chinese mind a qualitative association. That goes so far that I had great trouble at first in reading Granet, until I came to a story he tells, which is really so shocking that it woke me up. This is the story. There were once eleven generals who had to decide whether to attack or retreat in a battle. They held a meeting and some were for attacking and others for retreat. They had a long stregical discussion, and finally took a vote: three were for attacking and eight were for retiring, and they therefore decided to attack, because three is the number of unanimity!

You see, in China three has the quality of unanimity, and by the chance effect that three people were for attacking they hit the quality of the number three, therefore that opinion was the right one. A Chinese might say perhaps that underneath, unconsciously, there was unanimity for attack, despite the fact that only three were consciously for it, while eight were only unconsciously for it and consciously for another decision. Therefore they attacked — and successfully, according to the story.

From the point of view of our prejudices this is an absolutely crazy idea, but if you really let that story sink into your mind then you understand what a qualitative number is. In voting, for instance, the question is not which group is in the majority, but which group hits the right number, and their opinion counts. Suppose the number 1,566,000 is the number which expresses the true will of Switzerland and then we vote on something; it would be simply the group nearest to that number which won, quite apart from the fact that the others might be quantitatively more people. That is the twist in the Chinese mind and it is a good twist because it really shocks one out of the prejudice that number *can* only be a quantity. Number in the Chinese mind is a structure which has certain qualities.

In the I Ching, Hexagram 60, called *Chieh* (Limitation), says that limitlessness in life and everywhere in nature does not exist and is evil. Just as nature has its limitations — the stars have their courses, the tree does not grow beyond a certain height, everything in nature has its measure — so has human life, and therefore human life is only meaningful if it has also its meaningful limitations, its right measure. Therefore the Image for Hexagram 60 reads that "the superior man creates number and measure, and examines the nature of virtue and correct conduct." So there the idea of number has to do with virtue and the right attitude.

At the end of my last lecture I tried to explain that there is no objective quality in a deed — it depends on the measure and the time, and if it is done rightly within the limits of the personality. For the Chinese, virtue means doing the right things in the right measure at the right moment, and nowhere does one meet that idea as often as in analysis. If I tell a patient a truth today it may destroy him, but if I wait and tell him in three weeks' time it may help him. For everything there is the right moment, the right constellation for action, and to act too early or too late destroys the whole possibility. We do not consider that enough. We think too much in abstract terms, either that a thing is good or bad, and we do not think enough from the feeling standard of the special time circumstances in which we act, for our ethical deeds do depend on time.

The Chinese root of the word *Chieh* is the bamboo stick with knots, which shows very clearly how they saw it. A bamboo stick has certain knots, a rhythm, a limitation, a number, and the segments of a bamboo stick are the symbol for virtue, for loyalty, and for ethical order. Therefore the emperor was very often represented with such a bamboo stick because he was the conductor of the ethical concert of his people. Many texts in China say that if the emperor is not in order then the numbers of the empire and the numbers of the calendar fall apart. Then it is the task of the emperor to reinstate the right ethical rhythm, and by that also the order, the calendar — which the Chinese did quite concretely, for they had many calendar reforms and by them the emperor also restored the ethical order of his empire.

Here again number is associated with a moment in time. There is, so to speak, a one-moment, a two-moment, a three-moment, having to do with time and with ethical behaviour, which in our psychological language means with the feeling quality. Ethics are a question of feeling, not of the intellect. Very often, in many dreams, since my attention has been called to it, I have seen differentiation of feeling represented by a rainbow spectrum. If one has

84

very primitive feeling, then one has black and white reactions: I like it, or I don't like it, and there is nothing in between; or this is good and this is bad, agreeable or disagreeable — it is an either-or reaction. That is typical for undifferentiated feeling. Thinking types, for instance, react like that, while feeling types have a kind of spectrum of feeling reactions. A feeling type, if asked, "What do you think about Mrs. So-and-So?" will say, "Oh, well, on the one hand I have this impression and that impression and this criticism," and so on, and they give a whole rainbow spectrum of the personality, a spectrum of the different feelings they have towards the phenomenon of Mrs. So-and-So.

People who do not have differentiated feeling have dreams showing that they have to learn to differentiate it in this rainbow way, and not to have primitive all-or-none reactions. If one thinks of the legal world, which ultimately has so much to do with ethical problems, then one sees how important it is for a judge or a lawyer to have this differentiated spectrum by which to see the criminal. On the one hand the man is guilty and responsible for his deed, but on the other the circumstances have also to be considered, and in practice that is always done by us; finally one reaches a feeling judgement when all the pros and cons and nuances of the situation have been considered.

The Chinese went even further, having very much the same idea as the French, namely that really to understand is to be able to pardon the other person. They laid great weight on this feeling differentiation. The same is true for analytical work, for only if one can in a subtle way have a spectrum reaction — which means also not to be too sure of what is right and wrong, but can see all the different nuances, pros and cons — can one genuinely come to a human understanding. Feeling has a spectrum and a spectrum has different frequencies, so again there is a latent quantitative aspect to what is mainly qualitative.

In China, the rainbow is the symbol of Eros because it is what connects heaven and earth, which in China are the great principles of Yin and Yang; therefore the rainbow is a symbol of the feeling or Eros connection. There again comes the idea that feeling has a spectrum and a numerical order, and that there are, so to speak, feeling-time-numbers. That is what number is in China. How can we explain that?

I have tried to establish a polarity between the quantitative and

85

the qualitative number, but they must both have the same root in the human being and are really also secretly complementary aspects of one and the same thing. Here I have to call your attention to Jung's book *Symbols of Transformation*, where he first develops his energic viewpoint towards the psyche. He points out that eighty percent of the original manifestations of psychic energy in a small child are rhythmical movements with legs and arms and head, even when it produces its first sound: *popopopopo*. For hours a small child will amuse itself making bubbles and producing such rhythmical sounds.

Primitives too can only perform any kind of action if accompanied by such rhythmical movements, which is why they always drum or sing when they work. They cannot work on their own volition; they have to mobilize their psychic energy, their *gana*, as the South Americans, for instance, call it. If you ask a South American why he did not go to work, what is the matter, he will say: *"Mañana, today I have no gana."* If you cannot arouse his *gana* he will not do any work.

I have a neighbour in Bollingen who is still like that. He promised to do some building for me but never did it, and finally I went and sat with him and told him stories, and then he worked enthusiastically for nine hours straight. I had to give him the *gana*, to mobilize his psychic energy, and then he worked really well, but he was still like the South American Indians and we'd have the following conversation: "Oh, today I don't think I can come over." "Well, come, I have time today, couldn't you just see?" "Oh, no, I think the weather will be bad." "No, I don't think so, you see we could at least begin." "Well, let's look." "Couldn't you just take the shovel and your tools with you, just in case, you know . . ." And then he would come and work for hours and be very calm in the evening and say well we really had done something.

That is primitive mentality all over the world, for the great battle with the primitive is to get him out of his lethargy. When they know they have to do it by themselves, they do it by singing and drumming, which is why there are always initiation rituals before every action, whether hunting or sowing the fields; there always has to be a sort of chant and drum and ritual to arouse the *gana*, to excite the energy. The same is true of children, and it is one of the secrets of pedagogy. If there is a teacher among you I can tell you that that is the thing to do, for if you work up their *gana*, you can do anything with children; they are not lazy, they have the same trouble as a primitive does to get going. Once they are passionately involved they cannot stop.

So the original manifestation of psychic energy, when it becomes a cultural manifestation, is coupled with rhythm; it is not a random motor movement but a rhythmic movement. Jung says that this is the beginning of the spiritual form of instinct, that there the physiological aspect begins to have a spiritual form. Getting psychic energy to manifest rhythmically is the first form in which it manifests spiritually or culturally. In the animal kingdom it probably comes from the so-called displaced reaction. If you show a dog his food, he has all the Pavlovian reactions, his mouth waters, etc., but if you then pull the food away, he cannot turn off the whole thing; he was moved to eat, so he will sit down and scratch for half an hour. That is now well known and is what the zoologist calls a displaced reaction. The same thing happens if you show a horse his mate and then take the mare away — the horse will stamp for half an hour. Eighty percent of the displaced reactions in the animal kingdoms are rhythmical movements.

We too still have our apelike displaced reactions. When, for instance, people get impatient in a session, or there is a boring speaker, then they begin to scratch, or make rhythmical drawings with a pencil. That is the most primitive manifestation of free energy. So we can say that man was at first probably like the animals which live their instincts unconsciously: eating, mating, hunting, finding a place to live and defending the territory. Then a certain amount of energy was saved, and first manifested in the form of displaced reaction rhythms.

Jung points out in *Symbols of Transformation* that near the Amazon one finds rocks which have deep random cuts made by the Indios who sit there waiting for their canoes to be transported upstream. There is nothing for them to do, so with little sticks, or other stones, they make those little cuts all the time. They cannot wait quietly so they do that, and in time there are those deep cuts in the rocks. The oldest excavations we have from Middle Stone Age times in Europe are caves which have only recently been discovered. They are not the famous caves of Lascaux or Trois Frères, about which you have heard so much talk — most of which were discovered by the Abbé Breuille and which have those beautiful animal paintings, as well as points or designs by a medicine man or a shaman — but older caves discovered in Milly-la-Forêt.

These are in the middle of France in very inaccessible territory, and in them are deeply cut random lines — lines and lines and lines of them, exactly the same as the Indios still make on the rocks near the Amazon when they have to wait. So the Middle Stone Age men sat in those caves, probably when it rained or snowed, and they were unable to go hunting, and amused themselves with those rhythmical movements. That is probably the most primitive beginning of animal libido becoming free and beginning to transform itself into a cultural use.

In the Milly-la-Forêt caves there are other formations: for instance, regular arrangements of holes in rocks, with one that is famous, which the archaeologists call hollowed out stones; then there are triangles with a dot in the middle, and many simple mandala forms. One of these looks like the board for draughts, but it probably has nothing to do with the game. Later on somebody drew a picture of a stag in it.

Mrs. Marie König, who discovered these caves and who first published descriptions and photographed them, says also that she thinks (and she is not infected by Jungian psychology or anything like that) they were the very first attempts to establish a kind of ordered view of the universe of time and space — an attempt to establish time-space coordinates and some order in the confusing world of their surroundings. There one has an immediate connection between rhythm, rhythmical movement, and psychic energy mobilized to produce number and order.

Historically, that is probably the origin of the connection and one sees the extent to which number is absolutely connected with rhythm. In ancient Greece there is still something which points in that direction. The Greek word for number is *arithmos*, which as you all know the word arithmetic comes from, and rhythm is *rhythmos*; there is the same etymological root. So in the Greek word for number there is even preserved the idea that number was originally a rhythm, and, I would add, a psychic rhythm.

As always in China, very archaic ways of representation that have been shed in other civilizations have been preserved, which is why in that country up to the present time number is rhythm, a feeling rhythm, a harmony, a qualitative composition. For instance, in China one can say that the *ho* in music, or of a soup, is good, for the soup is also like a concert of various feeling reactions — good soup, with many flavours combined in it, is like a musical composition. *Ho* for the Chinese means musical harmony, and they use the word even to describe the quality of a meal. Here again is an illustration of the harmony of rhythm, in this case of taste impressions. I would therefore make the hypothesis that number has quantitative and qualitative aspects which are complementary, and that basically number expresses an energic rhythm which can be counted quantitatively, or experienced by feeling as a quality or a structure, and that was something which was known to certain Eastern people.

One of our former Japanese students, Dr. Mokusen Miyuki, called my attention to the fact that when Buddhism was first transplanted to China, there were different directions and different filiations of the original Buddha teaching. One of these filiations, typified as being very abstract and philosophical, was the so-called Hüa Yen Buddhism, and like the Zen Buddhists their traditions were transmitted by a series of patriarchs. The third patriarch of this tradition was a man called Fa Tzang, who developed a number theory in order to explain by mathematics how Buddha, according to tradition, preached a certain sutra in a state of deep sleep ecstasy. This was questioned by some intellectuals, who said: "How could the Buddha preach when he was in a deep sleep ecstasy? At such a time one would be in the Self where the awareness of the world or of other people has disappeared and therefore there should be no motivation to preach. If one was in ecstasy and in oneness with the Self, one would be silent and enjoy that in silence. How could one at that moment begin to preach as if there were still other people? For a man in that state other people do not exist."

That was a stupid, but not really a naive question, and Fa Tzang tried to explain by mathematics, saying that it meant the same relationship which the number one had to other numbers, namely that we cannot see things simultaneously, for either we are in the Self, and then there are no others, or we see others and are not in the Self, but we are possessed by it when we preach in awareness of others. Or, one is aware of the Self and then one does not see the others, but Buddha, in fact, was in a double state of mind where he paradoxically was in both states at the same time.

That, said Fa Tzang, could be explained by the fact that one

89

could look at number that way. He spoke of number in progression (Figure 13), pointing out that we count number in progression. He said that the number six or ten (he goes only up to ten) cannot exist without the one, of which it is really an aspect. But one should also look at number in regression and see that the ten is really a qualitative specification of the number one. Therefore one has to invent a retrograde form of counting, always referring back to the one and then one can understand what happened in Buddha: when he was turned to the others, he was as in the state of progression, looking at the many other selves in other people and trying to convert them, while at the same time, looking backwards, he was only in the one One.

$$1 \rightarrow 2 \rightarrow 3 \rightarrow 4 \rightarrow 5 \rightarrow 6 \rightarrow 7 \rightarrow 8 \rightarrow 9 \rightarrow 10 \quad \text{progression}$$
$$1 \leftarrow 2 \leftarrow 3 \leftarrow 4 \leftarrow 5 \leftarrow 6 \leftarrow 7 \leftarrow 8 \leftarrow 9 \leftarrow 10 \quad \text{regression}$$

Figure 13.

It is naturally a specification of the paradox of Indian philosophy that the personal Atman — the personal Self — and the superpersonal Atman are identical. That is so in the Upanishads. Many texts in the Upanishads say that if a man reaches his personal Self the Purusha within him is at the same time identical with the cosmic Self, and therefore one with all other people. So this oneness or otherness and its paradox plays a great role in the much older Indian philosophy, and this is only a late specification. I heard about Fa Tzang only after I had quite finished my book, but I was delighted to find a brother in spirit for my idea that we should now establish a mathematics of qualitative number.

Lancelot L. Whyte, whom I quoted before, said that before we can integrate the world of quality into the modern world of science, we must invent a new branch of mathematics with which to grasp it, and I think I see at least the beginnings of how that could come about. If we look at these qualitative numbers, as for instance the Chinese use them, then the 1, 2, 3, 4 are not different quantities but, as you know, time sequences of the same thing: one sees the wholeness first and afterwards the next facet, and then the next, but it is always the same one. The continuum is the continuation of the number one through the whole series (Figure 14), different aspects of the same number one, always the same, in a continuum underneath.

There are other mathematical concepts of the continuum,

which you should now not think of, for they are quantitatively defined. I am describing a different idea of the continuum from the one found in books of mathematics. This other view of the continuum we know already from the famous alchemical saying of Maria Prophetissa, which runs: "One becomes two, two becomes three, and out of the third comes the one as the fourth." You see she counts up to three and then says, but those are really all the one — she reconceives the oneness of the three and then puts them together as four. Our minds run progressively, for when we normally count, 1, 2, 3, 4, 5, we make a chain, while when we count qualitatively we can do the same thing and say now I have four. Yes, but the four is really the one continuum in the three, so I go backwards: four is a oneness of three, and I add that oneness to the three and make four, or five is the oneness of four, etc. That is what it actually is in China, for the five, in China, is not the next number after four, but it represents the oneness of the four, and four represents the oneness of the three.

The only place where I have found a similar way of counting in the Western world is in the speculation of the Trinity. A famous man, Joachino da Fiori, sincerely believed and understood that the Trinity was three hypostases of the Godhead but also that they were all one — not three separate persons but three hypostases of the same thing. So the Trinity, he said, has a common substance, and then he began to speak of the common substance as the fourth, but the pope condemned him for trying to introduce a heavenly quaternity instead of a Trinity. But he did it by counting: If the three are one, then there is a oneness of the three, and that oneness can be hypostatized separately and then one has the four. Maria Prophetissa also hypostatizes the three and gets the four.

There is the same thing in alchemy in the teaching of the quintessence. In the Middle Ages they did not believe that the quintessence was another element added to the other four; they thought that all nature consisted of four elements, and that the quintessence, the fifth, was the one of the four. In other words, there are

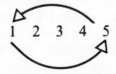

Figure 14. Number in progression —
the one-continuum.

91

four elements — water, fire, air, and earth — which have underneath a common substance, the quintessence. So again the four elements go back to their oneness and then hypostatize a fifth for the quintessence, the fifth essence.

There we see that our way of thinking is retrograde: we go back to the one again — that is generally the unconscious — and out of the process, the hypostatizing, we get to the fifth. So in our minds we do exactly the same thing as Fa Tzang, who thought that one should also count the numbers in regression.

Now comes an interesting fact. In all methods of divination, which to my idea are the primitive attempts of mankind to count psychic energy and its constellations, one counts backwards. In the I Ching fifty yarrow stalks are taken and one put aside. Then a bundle is taken and counted backwards until there is a remnant of either one, two, three, or four, so one literally counts backwards and it is the same in *all* divination methods which use numbers. For instance, in geomancy one takes a heap of corn and counts backwards until one has either an odd or an even remainder and that is used as information. So all the oracle methods, probably for a symbolic reason, use the idea of counting numbers in regression.

What I have described is a mental operation; namely, when I have the three I see them really as one, therefore it is the four, and then I say the four is really one if I try to think of getting to the five. Now that is a step in time of realization but it is only true for our conscious mind. In the unconscious there is a continuum where all are identical, just as the archetypes are identical. Or we could postulate that all numbers, being archetypal ideas, are in the unconscious identical, but if we want to reconstruct this or get a concept of it in our conscious mind, then we have to make the quality count in this retrograde form.

I found a beautiful example of this among the Navaho. I think it was Mrs. Baynes who gave me a modern tile of the Navaho, on which are the four goddesses of the Navaho pantheon (Figure 15). They have square heads, as you know, and a frock, and legs. Those four goddesses are represented in this way and then comes the amusing thing, for the fourth goddess is the first goddess reversed. That is a visualization of Maria Prophetissa's saying. From the one comes the two, from the two the three, and the one of the three is the fourth.

So that seems to be an archetypal way of reckoning — always at

92

a certain number to go back to the one and hypostatize it as the fourth. That is what Fa Tzang described as number in regression and is the kind of mathematics which most divination techniques use: one counts backwards to the original one, or two, and from that is drawn a conclusion.

If we think of it psychologically it is not at all crazy, because if we are in doubt, or in an uncertain situation, we are generally overwhelmed by the many aspects. One action will have this consequence and another that. We get confused and finally do not know where we stand. The desire is to get back to the one meaning, to the centre of oneself where there is only one meaning and one direction to go.

In geomancy, for instance, one takes a heap of pebbles absolutely at random — that is the confused manifold situation from which one can see no way out — and then one counts off two, two, two, two, and so on. Naturally, one can have a remainder of either one or two, because one has grabbed either an odd or an even amount of pebbles at random. This has to be repeated several times and from the result one concludes what one's situation is — expressed symbolically — and one gets away from the manifold confusion back to the original oneness of it all, its centre, as expressed by this symbolic or ritual gesture. That is why this retrograde way of counting is used.

Figure 15. Four Navaho primaeval
goddesses.

Richard Wilhelm, in his comments on the I Ching, explains this in another form, which I find very illustrative. Methods of divination are normally used to give a prognostication of the future and

93

the I Ching was also partly used in that way at first. Wilhelm explains the idea of the Chinese when he says that if we knew how a tree contracted into a seed, then we could predict the future. This is like saying that if we can understand the retrograde process of development then we can predict the future. There is the same thing in the word *Suan chi lai*, which means to enumerate the origin of what will happen. One enumerates backwards to the origin of what will happen. The Chinese say the future is always present as a seed, so if I know how a tree contracts to a seed then I can also predict how the tree will develop from the seed. If we know the kernel point of a situation we can predict its consequences.

Now what that means in psychological language is that if we know the deepest underlying archetypal constellation of our present situation then we can, to a certain extent, know how things will go. Archetypal dreams are valid on an average for from three to six months — but perhaps for ten years, or a whole lifetime. It depends on the greatness of the dream. Dreams from the personal unconscious are valid for about three days. That is why very often during an analysis somebody has a sequence of personal material, shadow dreams, which are everyday reactions to the everyday attitude, and one works on that and then suddenly, like a cut, into it comes a big archetypal dream. One interprets it and the patient cannot make head nor tail of it and says: "Yes, but how does that connect with my situation? I am impressed and feel somewhere that it is a very deep dream but I see no connection with my present situation." In my experience one has to say, "Wait," for it usually takes between two or three months for such a situation to be full-blown, a conscious reality. Then generally inner events occur and sometimes synchronistic outer events, and after three months, on looking back, one can say: "Ah, I see now what that dream meant." It has taken all that time to come up, and the deeper the dream the longer it takes. In that way one gets to the deepest constellation and one can predict the future.

The Chinese idea is that if one knows the very deepest constellation then one knows the constellation which will still be valid in two or three years, and it is so practically. That is why Jung got so interested in children's dreams; the earliest dream of a child sometimes anticipates the whole life. That is like the seed: one looks into a child's dream and sees the seed of a life which later will be a full-grown tree. One already sees the seed in the child's archetypal dream when two or three years old. One could therefore say that really what we do in psychology is also to count retrograde, and I think that is what really pushed Freud to put such an emphasis on early childhood experience. He was really inspired by this idea, but he put it into the conscious, and only into the outer events of childhood, instead of into the archetypal constellation. The childhood dream is the seed of a whole fate, a whole *Schicksal* sometimes, and if you can read that pattern then you can, to a certain extent, read the future of this life pattern. One cannot be specific, but one can in general read the pattern. From these experiences the Chinese invented this retrograde counting method when they used numbers for divination.

We come now to another aspect. I have noticed, as have some of you, I know, that I have to some extent contradicted myself. Let us go back to the number arrangement. Sometimes I have said that numbers, qualitatively, are the one continuum which only in the time sequence develops other aspects but is always the same thing; and then I have used retrograde counting methods which treat numbers again as discrete, as a discontinuous entity — the three was something different from the four, and so on. That has to do with the relative timelessness of the deeper layers of the unconscious. As you know, Jung thinks that the deepest layers of the unconscious, which would mean especially the collective unconscious layers in the psyche, are relatively timeless, i.e., outside time and space. As I just mentioned, in a childhood dream sometimes the whole fate of a person is already present; the future is, so to speak, present in the unconscious. But as a conscious experience it may take that human being more than twenty, thirty, or sixty years to realize it, so we must assume that certain archetypal constellations are relatively eternal. I would not like to say eternal, because so far we can only observe that they are relatively timeless, while our conscious mind — discursive thinking and all the processes in consciousness — are time-bound. The time concept, whatever it means, is certainly bound to the flow of energy in consciousness, for our conscious processes follow one after another.

There are times when the unconscious does not follow that order, for instance in the way certain mathematicians discover their theories. Henri Poincaré describes how he worked for weeks and weeks on a problem involving what are now called automorphous functions. (I will not try to explain it because I do not understand it myself, it is complicated higher mathematics.) He could not find the solution and then went to military service. One evening when he was very tired he drank some coffee and afterwards could not sleep, and suddenly he saw, as he describes it himself, how ideas and combinations flew about like atoms in space and combined and disconnected again and suddenly made the right kind of connection, and he saw the whole solution! In one flash! He got up but it took him over half an hour to develop the course of the proof and write it out. The conscious mind needed half an hour of one argument after another: from that follows that, and from that follows that, till he finally had the proof that made him famous in the world of mathematics — but he *saw* it in one flash.

The same is true for the famous mathematician Gauss. He found one of the number theorems in the same way. He said: "My mind was engrossed with the problem but I could not see the solution and then suddenly, by the grace of God, in a flash of lightning I saw the whole thing, but even afterwards I could not say how I got there, or how I argued, and what the connection was." He saw the whole order timelessly so to speak, but then his conscious mind had to work along the threads of connection and transform it into mathematical proof, which consists of a first, second, third, and fourth step, and so on.

All such hints point to the fact that in the unconscious there is not this sequence of "one after another." That is the way to which our conscious mind is bound — through time and space — it is the only way in which our minds can function, but somehow in the unconscious time and space become relative or, if they do not vanish, at least they become very flexible, they are no longer valid as in our conscious.

The Chinese, therefore, when they tried to describe the totality of the universe, fell on the idea of making two orders. You remember the *Lo Shou* and the *Ho-tou*. The *Ho-tou* is connected with what they call the eternal order of the universe, in which heaven and earth are opposite each other, with the elements arranged accordingly. That is a mandala of a certain form, in which all the archetypal possibilities are arranged, an archetypal field which they call the eternal order and in which they say the elements are in energic connection but do not fight and do not move. That would mean, for instance, that there is fire and water, and they have a kind of energy tension between each other as in a magnetic field, but they do not move or rotate, they are in a kind of animated stillness. If you want a poetic simile you could compare it to the dragonfly, which can hover in midair like a helicopter while making very frequent wing movements; it moves but remains completely stationary, and that is how one could imagine this order. It is full of tension and inner vibration, but as a whole it is still and therefore does not enter time or space.

The second mandala the Chinese made to describe the order of the universe is what they call the Younger Heavenly Order. That is built up mathematically on the *Lo Shou*, so it is said to move cyclicly, in a time-cycle. In China, as in India, they had the idea of a cycle, a cyclical time movement. To imagine time as a cyclic movement and not as a linear movement is typically Eastern. So one order is time-bound and the other not, it is eternal. They are called the Older and the Younger Heavenly Orders.

One of the oldest forms of divination was to draw the eternal, the Older Heavenly Order, on a round plank, representing heaven, and the Younger on a square one, supposed to represent the earth. Through a hole in the middle of each they put a stick. They rotated the two against each other and then let them come to rest, and from the way those two combined, as in roulette, they read the situation.

That is one of the very oldest forms of divination; it has only recently been excavated in China and is probably even older than the I Ching. What seems most important to me is the idea of two systems interacting and by that representing totality.

Lecture 5

In his paper on synchronicity Jung stresses the point that since the physical and the psychic realms coincide within the synchronistic event, there must be somewhere or somehow a unitarian reality — one reality of the physical and psychic realms to which he gave the Latin expression *unus mundus*, the one world, a concept which already existed in the minds of some mediaeval philosophers. This world, Jung says, we cannot visualize, and it completely transcends our conscious grasp. We can only conclude, or assume, that there is somewhere such a reality, a psycho-physical reality we could call it, which sporadically manifests in the synchronistic event. Later, in *Mysterium Coniunctionis,* he says that the mandala is the inner psychic equivalent of the *unus mundus.*

This would mean, as you know, that the mandala represents an ultimate oneness of inner and outer reality. It points to a transcendental psychological content which we can only indirectly grasp through symbols. The many forms of the mandala seem to point to that oneness, the synchronistic events being the parapsychological equivalent of the *unus mundus* and also pointing to this same oneness of the psychic and physical universe. Therefore it is not surprising that we should find combinations of those two motifs in history, namely of the mandala structures and past attempts in divination to grasp synchronicity. I call these mandalas divinatory mandalas.

There are many techniques of divination in which a mandala is the instrument, the most well known being the horoscope and the transit horoscope. I have already outlined the two world orders of the Chinese which were designed on two planchettes and rotated against each other for divination purposes. There are many other

98

such mandalas which we also find in antiquity; for instance, in antique medicine they had so-called spheres of divination. One took the age of the patient, the day and the month and the position of the moon when he became ill, and rotated that information in the mathematical mandala until the prognosis was reached. If the numerical results fell on the lower part of the spheres the patient would die; if they fell on the upper parts then he would recover.

Those circles or spheres were also used for divination in general. For instance, if a slave had run away one could ask whether he would come back or be found, or if he was lost forever. One used the same method, namely one took the age of the slave, the day he had run away and a few other numbers; these were recorded in those spheres and according to where the results fell one thought one had information about the outcome of the situation.

These rather absurd techniques show that in the background of the minds of the people who invented them was the idea that the possible knowledge one could have about such events was connected with the *unus mundus,* which would explain why they drew them in mandala form.

The most striking thing is that whenever mandalas were used for divination they were frequently *double* mandala structures; namely, two wheels intercepting each other, one wheel generally being fixed and representing one aspect of reality, and the other wheel rotating over the fixed wheel, the combination of the two being used for divination. These double mandalas in China (we have them too), which rotate against each other, as I mentioned before, are the Older Heavenly Order, an arrangement of the sixty-four possibilities or permutations of the hexagrams of the I Ching, and the Younger Heavenly Order which had a different arrangement of the same I Ching trigrams and hexagrams. In the Older Heavenly Order there are no energic temporal processes but a kind of dynamism in balance with itself, while in the Younger Heavenly Order a cyclic energic process is represented.

Jung, in his paper on synchronicity, also came to the conclusion that synchronistic events are not just sporadic irregular happenings, without any order. At the end of the paper he advances the hypothesis that they are random phenomena of what he calls acausal orderedness. In other words, we would have to assume that in psychic as well as in physical reality there is a kind of timeless order or orderedness which always remains constant, and synchronistic events fall into the area of these events of which they are single sporadic actualizations.

As an example of acausal order in the physical world, Jung mentions radioactive decay and its constant temporal order. He calls it acausal because we have no possibility of explaining causally why radioactive decay should occur in this numerical order and not in another form. It is, so to speak, a just-so story. As an example of the constancy of acausal orderedness in the psychic realm he mentions the qualities of the natural integers. We cannot for instance say why, or causally explain why, certain integers are prime numbers and why they are arranged the way they are; that too is a just-so story, just a fact which we cannot refer back to a cause. The question why, or where that comes from, is irrelevant in that moment, one can only say that is how it is.

That is what Jung understands by acausal orderedness. It means certain orders in the mental and physical realms which are its best expression. It is a just-so story. What is more striking is that it is absolutely constantly so, there are no individual deviations or variations. We can assume, therefore, that in nature there is a certain amount of acausal orderedness, certain orders which physical and psychic nature keep, thus producing by those constant events a constant order. Synchronistic events would be manifestations of this acausal orderedness, but in contradistinction to events which are regular and therefore completely predictable, the synchronistic event happens within that order but is unique, sporadic, and unpredictable.

When Jung first put forward his hypothesis of the principle of synchronicity, there was much discussion as to whether one could not still discover a law under which synchronistic events would have a certain regularity, or would follow certain laws and therefore become predictable so that one could say now, in that situation, a synchronistic event *must* happen. This it has not been possible to find and Jung, after long reflection and discussion, came to the conclusion that we have to admit, much as it annoys our rational minds, that synchronistic events are just-so stories.

But one might ask: why on earth then has mankind from the very beginning always tried to invent methods to predict synchronicity? To which one could reply that that was the primitive mind which confused synchronicity and causality; i.e., people really wanted to predict in a causal way but because they did not think clearly, in

100

their muddled minds they had a kind of magic conception of synchronicity and causality and therefore assumed that one could predict. That might be true to a certain extent, but if one watches more closely what happens in the different techniques of divination one sees that actual events are never predicted, but only the *quality* of *possible* events.

For instance, in astrology, if a very old person has an extreme number of negative constellations in his transit horoscope, an astrologer might hazard a guess that he will probably succumb, so that one could speak of possible death. I have discussed that with several astrologers who all confirm that one cannot, for example, predict the death of a person from a horoscope, one can only say there seems to be a very difficult constellation and that if the person is already old and sick there is the possibility that at this date death will occur.

If you are familiar with the technique of throwing the I Ching you will see that it too does not predict what actually happens — it only says "unexpected bad luck" or something like that, and then something will happen within that area, but it cannot predict that you will get a letter from your mother saying she will not send any more money. I mean you do not read that in the I Ching, you only read "unexepected bad luck" or something similar. In other words, the prediction only refers to the quality of the moment in which a synchronistic event might occur. That is why, for instance, diviners and medicine men, etc., never swear that something will inevitably happen, but say there is only the likelihood or possibility that something in this area will happen.

The same thing holds good even for prognostic dreams. Just the other day a friend of mine told me that many years ago, when he was doing a lot of mountaineering, he had a dream before going on an expedition that a stone avalanche would kill him. On waking up in the morning he was very much concerned and debated whether he should put off the expedition or not, but then felt that if he did that he would feel like a coward and would be ashamed of himself. Also he was probably tickled by curiosity to find out if it would happen or not. So he decided to go all the same but to take a second guide, which was of no use at all, as you will soon see, but that was his idea of taking precautions. Actually he went on the climb and nothing happened — except that on the way back a stone avalanche came down and just missed them by so much. The second guide would not have helped at all, they would all have been killed. So the unconscious was not able to predict quite accurately what was going to happen, but it predicted an accident in the mountains and then there was a little just-so on this or that side which could not be predicted. Only a likelihood was predicted in the dream.

It looks, therefore, as if the absolute knowledge of the deeper layers of our unconscious psyche cannot predict synchronistic and other events quite accurately, but can sketch a more or less blurred image of possibilities. This is also what divination techniques attempt: they do not define or predict the possible synchronistic event, because that is really unpredictable, but only sketch, with the help of acausal orderedness, the quality of a time moment. So one can say that if something happens it will fall into the area of this qualitative field. For instance, "accident in the mountains" would in the above case be the general slogan and therefore it would not likely mean a marvellous encounter with a chamois, but something would happen in the area of an accident in the mountains. The unconscious expectation was turned in that area but the actual event and how it would actually take place was not predictable. That is true for all divination techniques.

This leads us to the problem of time, and it is interesting to see that even in modern physics some physicists have arrived at similar problems. The French physicist, Costa de Beauregard, tries to solve the problem without knowing anything about Jung. I wrote and asked him if he knew Jung's work and he wrote back that he only knew Freud's but after what I told him was going to read Jung. So his theory has come out completely independent of Jungian ideas. De Beauregard is a professor of physics at the Sorbonne in Paris; he belongs to the group of relativists among the physicists, and is specially concerned with the problem of time.

The title of de Beauregard's book is *Le Second Principe et la Science du Temps.* In it he comes to the conclusion that there are two areas of reality and therefore two types of time. One type is the actual physical reality, as physicists know it, in which time is generally represented by a parameter; that means time is conceived as linear. It is the same model of thought as I gave in the beginning of my lecture about causality. We conceive time as such a line of events and therefore represent it in physical models of reality through a linear parameter. This, de Beauregard says, is closely linked to our consciousness, while the actual world in the relativist sense of the word is a four-dimensional world which is timeless. Only our consciousness walks along world lines so the linear time phenomenon is bound to our consciousness, and with it also probability in the physical sense of the word and the principle of irreversibility.

In other words, because of entropy there is a certain loss of energy in every process so that in every event the goal is of a lower energy potential than the beginning stage. This means that energy in the universe "runs down," so to speak, towards entropy; the irreversibility of all actual events, as observable in consciousness, makes for the fact that time is linear, that there is a course of events, so to speak, which is irreversible. Then de Beauregard asks the question whether there is not also another area of reality in which the contrary aspect is true.

Physicists have all sorts of strange projections about this. Some, for instance, imagine that far, far away, somewhere else in the universe, there is a world of "anti-matter" where all the processes we can watch in our world are reversed. Nobody has proved or observed that world, it is just a mental image based on the notion of symmetry or balance — the feeling that if we live in a world where everything runs down energically, there must somewhere be a place where energy is built up.

De Beauregard has another idea, namely, that a four-dimensional world, in the Minkowski-Einsteinian sense of the word, is identical with the unconscious and this he calls an "elsewhere." In this timeless elsewhere, this *ailleurs,* are processes in which the opposite takes place, i.e., systems of higher energy charge are built up. This four-dimensional elsewhere participates in the world of information or of imagery representation. In other words, for him this elsewhere is something psychic, something unconscious, and something in which representations are built up. He also calls it information, but he defines information as mental representation. This built-up world is complementary to the physical world where everything runs down, and has systems of higher energy charge than those in our physical world. He explains that this makes it possible for man — who takes part in this psychological *ailleurs,* this world of representations — by acts of volition himself to interrupt the course of nature and build up systems of higher order again. In this way, by making use of his psychic background, man could in effect reverse "irreversible" processes in the physical world. At the end of his book he alludes

103

to this other world of a psychic order, in which systems of higher energy charges are built up, and says that it is identical with his idea of God.

There are all sorts of points, when one looks at this theory of de Beauregard, which to my mind are very tenuous. I am not at all convinced, but I would say that it is a kind of intuitive concept which comes very near to what Jung calls "the collective unconscious." What de Beauregard describes as this four-dimensional elsewhere, in which representations are built up and from which energy is then drawn to interfere with outer physical events, is what we would define as the collective unconscious. He got there through a kind of intuitive similar idea. Where it seems to me to be a bit questionable is where — because he has a Catholic education or background — he describes this elsewhere, for him the world of the Godhead, as something purely good, beneficent, benevolent, and so on, and there we would put a question mark. Also it is a purely intuitive theory, as he gives no actual evidence for his ideas. But we see that even in modern physics there are now developments, mainly concerned with the problem of time, which are leading physicists to ideas and discoveries similar to a Jungian viewpoint.

Another man I would like to mention is a Jewish French mathematician and physicist, Albert Lautmann, who was shot by the Nazis at the age of 32. He must have been a very intelligent person, but unfortunately he published only a single book on the principle of symmetry and asymmetry in nature. He develops a theory of two times: linear time, which could be represented mathematically by a parameter, say a line, and another time which he calls cosmogonic time. The latter he conceives of as a field in which he says "topological accidents would take place." He tried to invent a mathematical model to describe time by two factors; namely, by a linear factor on the one hand and a field factor on the other. That naturally verges on the mathematical angle, but is not the same thing, as I tried to describe before — though there are certain striking parallel ideas, namely that we could conceive of the natural integers as a continuum field. Of course he uses algebra and geometry and does not refer to the natural integers. His field of topological accidents would, from my standpoint, be another intuitive hypothesis which approaches my idea of the collective unconscious conceived of as a one continuum field ordered by the rhythms of the archetypes.

What de Beauregard has not at his disposition and which we can add, is that, for us, the archetypes would be "engines," so to speak, to produce higher energy loads. As Jung has expressed it, the archetype is a phenomenon which produces energy and is therefore, one might say, negentropic; it is a negentropic phenomenon and there we could dispute with Costa de Beauregard and say the *ailleurs* which really creates the higher states of energy, is not what he calls representations. He is quite vague about whether the representations are conscious or unconscious — he constantly makes no distinction between the two — but we would say that our conscious representations are not engines which make higher charges of energy. Not at all. With our theory of archetypes, however, we can prove that there *are* such dynamic centres which produce psychic energy, and secondarily the representations of which de Beauregard speaks. There he has just not differentiated enough, not knowing of our investigations.

What seems to me important is that if we look psychologically at Albert Lautmann's mathematical theory or de Beauregard's physical theory, we see that there has been an endeavour to construct a kind of double mandala, but in the form of a theory of two complementary systems: one time-bound and one which contains an eternal order. Modern physicists are concerned with the problem of time, so they fall back to the idea of the double mandala. They do not express it that way, but one sees that their theory corresponds to that old pattern of thought, to a double concept of time.

The problem of double motifs has also another aspect. If you remember, Jung points out that he discovered while he was writing his paper on synchronicity that, usually, dreams with double motifs seem to refer to the problem of synchronicity. He tells some of his own dreams and some of other people and they always follow the same pattern: one finds something impossible in nature and either there is a doubling of something impossible in reality, or a coincidence of two incommensurable facts.

In one dream, for instance, a dream of a woman, the woman finds in a cave, which has been discovered but where no human had ever been, patterns on the wall which look man-made. It was as if nature herself had made the drawings, the heads, and so on; they had all the characteristics of being man-made though objectively that was not possible. In another dream the dreamer sees a one-cellular cockerel, in the tundra in northern Russia. Jung concludes that such dreams point to the possibility of something apparently

105

impossible — things which are absolutely impossible according to our conscious view of nature, but which from the standpoint of the unconscious actually exist. Very often there is the motif, for instance, of artefacts being made which we think only the human psyche can produce, e.g., such carvings in a cave, which are produced there by nature. Jung took those dreams to point to the principle of synchronicity, namely that in the synchronistic event two factors which are inconceivably one coincide or become one.

I have noticed the same in my own unconscious. When I was grappling with these problems I had a dream that I was in a train with many mathematicians. I just went to say goodbye to them but the conductor called out: "If you want to get off that train hurry up, because it is just leaving." So at the last minute I jumped off the train, which was already moving. The mathematicians had gone, so now what? Then I came to a table on which were fragments of excavations of an old Hindu civilization. It was the usual museum stuff. There were little fragments of pottery, one could not figure out at all what they really were but one felt awed by them because they were so old. They were not very attractive, I must admit, but among them was a crystal glass with a figure on it of a youth holding grapes, a figure of Dionysus, or a Dionysus-like god. That would refer to the living spirit of nature.

Then I went on and up the mountains where I saw, as one usually does in the high Swiss mountains, brown wooden huts, some with little gardens round them with just a few carrots, etc., for the people who watch the cattle up there. The entrances to the gardens were always marked by two stones. People often mark entrances by two stones, or stone pillars such as were there, but now comes the amazing thing. The two stones were ordinary field stones picked up at random and of irregular form, but there were always two of them and inside there was a mathematical pattern of golden threads. *The two stones and patterns were completely identical.* They had not been cut apart to make two alike, they were two different stones, picked up individually, each of which had this absolutely identical pattern, something completely impossible in nature. I just stared at these stones in awe and amazement that such an impossible thing should be.

That was just another dream comparable to the dreams Jung tells in his paper on synchronicity. They show, as Jung points out, that there must be a formal factor in nature which coordinates, so to speak, certain forms in the physical world with the psychic world, two incompatible worlds. Later he often pointed out that if people dream of such impossible things it generally means that they have a too-rational outlook on reality, and the unconscious wants to show that there *is* something miraculous which does not obey the laws of nature as we now rationally conceive them — there is something beyond that. What is also striking is that there is a double motif which contains an element of symmetry such as in these double mandalas which are symmetrical to each other.

Double motifs, as we usually interpret them, refer in general to the fact that something is just coming up to the threshold of consciousness. If somebody dreams of two identical dogs, or identical people, etc., it means this content is just coming up from the unconscious and approaching the threshold of consciousness; at the threshold it falls apart into two. I think that is why we also have at all boundary lines this idea of placing double stones, double pillars, and so on. We always use a double marker at the threshold; it is a symbolic urge suggesting that the threshold of consciousness is a doubling phenomenon, so to speak, all of which would point to the fact that what we call time is an archetypal idea, not yet properly conscious to us. We do not yet know what time really is, and the moment has apparently come when the archetype of the concept of time is approaching the threshold of consciousness.

As far as I can see there is everywhere this idea of two orders, which I will now call, as Jung does, acausal orderedness on the one side, which is timeless, and synchronistic events, which enter linear time, on the other side. Now comes the great problem — how are those two things connected? How is the *ailleurs* of de Beauregard connected with his physical everyday world? How is the cosmogonic time of Lautmann connected with the linear parameter time? How is the principle of acausal orderedness, which belongs to the world of physics and the collective unconscious according to Jung, connected with the world of time and space, as we can only conceive it in our consciousness?

Since we have no other information available at the moment, we can only look at the products of the unconscious, namely the double mandalas, and see how they are connected. The interesting thing is that such double mandalas are usually represented as wheels, two wheels, or two discs, but generally wheels (Figure 16). If you were to cut that diagram out in cardboard and try to make such a thing, you would see that those wheels cannot rotate, but would destroy each other. In spite of it all, these double mandala models assume that one wheel is rotating and the other standing still, but if one wheel rotated it would cut the other wheel apart and vice versa, and if both rotated there would just be an explosion which would destroy everything. I mean that mechanically those two wheels cannot rotate.

So all these symbolic references to the meeting of those two worlds seem to show that the world of time and the world of acausal orderedness outside time, are two incompatible systems that cannot be put together but are complementary. They are, that is, more than complementary — they are incompatible and we cannot imagine how they are linked to each other, which is probably also the reason why we cannot establish any law of synchronicity, for then the wheels would have to be coordinated in a certain way.

The only place where the two systems link is at the hole in the centre, which means that they link in a nowhere, or in a hole. This mysterious hole between the two worlds is in a one-sided way also represented in the Chinese incense clock. The Chinese had very accurate clocks before they became acquainted with our clock systems, but on a completely different principle. They drew a mandala in labyrinth form into which they put a thread such as one would use for a time bomb, or some powder which has the same quality as the fuse of a time bomb, namely that it burns on and on for a

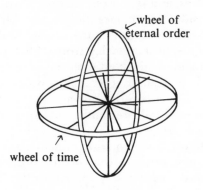

Figure 16. Double mandalas — two
sorts of time.

108

certain time. This they lit and covered up and it went on smouldering, and to find the time one just opened the lid and looked to see
what point the fire had reached and that was the time. They even
invented alarm clocks in that way — to certain parts of this smouldering thread they attached a pebble and put the clock above their
heads when they went to sleep, and when the smouldering thread
had reached this point the pebble dropped on their heads and woke
them. This is still used in China, for where they have no other clocks
they have these incense clocks, as they are called, and according to
Joseph Needham they are fairly accurate and completely satisfactory for practical life.

Here the interesting fact is that time in China is conceived of as
a field in which a patterned energic process takes place, and accordingly they invented this device which works in the form of a clock.
There too there is a hole, where the smoke escapes and where the
thread is inserted. Time therefore has a hole where man interferes,
where man steps into the picture. There is no absolute time. It is
the same with our clocks: some have to be wound up, or now we
have another technique by which our own movement winds them
up, but if the watch is not used, if it is put on a desk and left, it
will not go. So at the hole in time, in measured time, *man steps in.*
That is only a little analogy, on the technical level, of a much deeper problem, namely this hole of eternity.

In the Middle Ages the anima, or matter as the anima, was also
identified with the Virgin Mary and there are many alchemical
texts and also certain official ecclesiastical hymns in which the
Virgin Mary is called "the window of eternity," or "the window of
escape." According to our modern definition the anima figure is,
in a man, the bridge between the personal and the collective unconscious, and there also she carries the title of the window of
escape, or the window of eternity.

In *Mysterium Coniunctionis,* Jung at the end quotes extensively
from the work of an alchemist, Gerhard Dorn, in whose philosophy
the window of eternity or the *spiraculum aeternitatis* also plays a
great role. *Spiraculum* is an air hole, through which eternity breathes
into the temporal world. We see therefore that this meeting place,
which is a vacuum, is an archetypal representation which in mythological and alchemical philosophy appears as the place where the
personal realm of the psyche, including the personal unconscious,
touches the collective unconscious. It is as though the collective

109

unconscious were the eternal order and the personal unconscious and personal conscious would together be the time-bound order, their connection being through the hole.

Jung interprets this *spiraculum aeternitatis,* this air-hole, or breathing hole into eternity, as the experience of the Self. He says that through the experience of the Self we can escape and be freed from the grip of a one-sided image of the world.

Now, reality is only real in so far as we are conscious of it. It is consciousness, therefore, which casts for us the image of the reality in which we move all the time, and that is a cage, or a prison. The hole, which is the experience of the Self, breaks that cage or prison of our conscious reality apart and by that frees us from the grip of its one-sided concepts. This hole, therefore, seems to be like a pivot, the point at which the two systems meet. The Chinese philosopher Mo Dsi has, to my mind, amplified what that means in practical psychological language. He says in *The Doctrine of the Mean:*

> Only the man who is devoted to utmost sincerity can unfold his own nature completely, and through that he can also unfold the nature of his surroundings completely, and thus can support the transforming and nourishing powers of heaven and earth. Only a man devoted to complete inner sincerity can know the future. This virtue is really a quality of nature and thus [that means if a man can know the future and is possessed by the utmost sincerity] *a union of the outer and inner can take place* and the ways of heaven and earth can be explained in one sentence. *They are without any doubleness* and that is how they produce things in an unfathomable way.

So heaven and earth, Yin and Yang, are united in China through such a hole and they too meet in this innermost meeting point where "there is no doubleness." You see in the central point of the diagram (Figure 16) there is no doubleness; everywhere else there is, but in this point there is oneness. This place of oneness is the point where heaven and earth unite and also the place where creation takes place. From this hole comes creation, from this nowhere comes everything which is newly created.

I want to remind you here that Jung defined synchronistic events as an act of creation. A synchronistic event is an acausal event and is therefore, one could say, an act of creation. Jung believed in a *creatio continua,* like certain modern physicists who believe that there is in the world in which we live a place where from time to time new things are created. The synchronistic event would be such an act of creation. That is naturally self-evident for the Chinese mind, because they think only in synchronistic terms, and creative acts, which are synchronistic events, come from this hole where heaven and earth meet. Then comes this beautiful Chinese idea that man can actually get in contact with that—he can get to the place where heaven and earth create in an unfathomable way, without doubleness, through utmost sincerity. If somebody devoid of all illusions, and all that makes the world of the ordinary ego, goes into himself with utmost sincerity, then he comes to this central hole where creation, even in the cosmos, takes place. That is why the Chinese thought that certain sages or saints, very rare personalities, could reach that centre and by having come to this contained innermost centre of their personality could support heaven and earth, and be with creation in the universe.

We find this archetypal motif in another area of divination which I now want to mention briefly because it is also such beautiful material. In his paper on synchronicity Jung mentions the divination art of geomancy. Geomancy is a "terrestrified" astrology. Instead of taking the constellations of the stars and using them for divination, one makes the constellations of the stars oneself on earth ($g\bar{e}$ means earth) and then proceeds as in astrology. As I mentioned before, a handful of pebbles or corn is taken, and then paired off, leaving at the end an odd or an even number with which one makes figures and builds up something similar to the trigrams of the I Ching. From these quaternios one makes an astrological chart to be read according to certain rules, as with a horoscope.

I can refer you to an excellent paper written by K. Josten in *The Journal of the Warburg & Courtauld Institute,** on Robert Fludd's *Theory of Geomancy* and Josten's experiences at Avignon in the winter of 1961-62. Robert Fludd, a contemporary of Keppler, with whom he had a famous *Auseinandersetzung,* was one of those who still believed in this art of geomancy and what is remarkable about him is that he tried to make a psychological theory about it. He did not just use geomancy for prognostication in a magical, primitive way, but he thought about it. Jung says in his paper on synchronicity that unfortunately geomancy, which would be the Western equivalent of what the I Ching is to Asia, has never been developed into an all-encompassing philosophy as has the I Ching. It has been used mostly only for primitive prognostication and that is true

---

*Vol. 97, 1964, p. 327.

even for Fludd, who experimented with it only to find out if he should marry Mrs. So-and-So or not, and if he would have money or not. He never got further than that but he tried to make an interesting psychological theory about it.

There is still another place on this planet where geomancy has been philosophically developed to something which seems to me to have a value nearly equivalent to the Chinese I Ching, and that is by the medicine men of Western Nigeria. They learnt the art of geomancy through the Northern Islamic people. Geomancy was practised in India, and in the whole Islamic civilization, and from there came to Europe in the 10th or 11th century, at the same time as alchemy and all the other natural sciences. But it also migrated south and got into the hands of certain Western Nigerian medicine men. This marvellous material is to be found in a book by Bernard Maupoil entitled *La Géomancie à l'ancienne Côte des Esclaves* (Paris, 1943). This book gives a complete explanation of the technique of geomancy, especially as practised by these African medicine men; it is the same as was practised in North Africa by the Islamic civilization.

These medicine men have an interesting belief that is part of the tradition of their art of divination: it was thanks to a god called Fa that the geomantic oracle gave a true answer and not due to the mechanisms of the divination technique. This god Fa is worshipped by different tribes, the Mina, the Fon, the Yoruba, etc. These populations have a polytheistic religion and many different benevolent and malevolent demons who have collective cults which are in this country called voodoo, but the god Fa, the father of the oracle, is not a voodoo and does not belong to the pantheon of these tribes for the following reason: a voodoo can always produce trance or possession and can work good and evil. Remnants of this also exist in variations among the natives of Haiti, where they still go into trance and get possessed by certain voodoos and express what they do. Fa, the god of this oracle, in contrast to a voodoo, never works black magic. He only tells an individual the truth, and only the individual to whom he tells the truth can know that it is the truth and can know what it is. Fa has no collective power — the god when he manifests only addresses unique individuals and tells them something which is uniquely true only for that individual and for nobody else. Therefore he has no cult, no priests, nothing, because he is simply that power of truth.

There is here a certain similarity to the idea of Mo Dsi, that there is a power of inner truth which is creative and which works in these things. The god Fa came from a country called Ifé, the country from which mankind came and to which the dead return. You know that the world which I have called the *unus mundus* is, in all primitive mythologies, the land of the dead; the dead live in the *unus mundus,* or in that transcendental world, in that Beyond, and that is the land Ifé. Fa comes from there and therefore, because he is the god of truth, the Nigerian says it is only when you die that you will discover the secret of life. As long as you live in this temporal world you never know the pattern of your life, you live from minute to minute trying to find it; but at the moment of death you have the whole pattern, you see it from the other world. So only when you die do you discover the secret of life. God created the world and He did not do only good things, He also created evil. Fa is the only power which does not want evil, so he is different from God. God wants good and evil and creates good and evil. Fa is only benevolent to man, is only sincere, and only creates the good. Each living human being has an invisible soul, which the Fon call Ye, the life principle or soul, but man does not understand the meaning of his Ye. Whoever seeks to know the secret of his life should therefore go to Fa, who is called Fa because he is himself the only Ye (soul principle) which can reveal the truth of the greatness of life.

The word Fa comes from the freshness of water and air. There one must remember that in hot Africa fresh water and fresh air are an incredibly positive experience, for if one has been in the heat and gets to a palm grove and finds a spring, it is like finding life. Fa is the freshness of the water. We have, by the way, in the Catholic church a similar representation, for one name for Paradise is *refrigerium,* the place of refreshment, and in Catholic parlance that represents inward peace. These Nigerian tribes say, therefore, that every difficulty, however hot, can become cool and quiet through contact with Fa, and then it is easier to bear.

We know from our own experience that the worst neurotic sufferings come from being entangled with ourselves and our own complexes, and if we have enough sincerity in the sense of Mo Dsi to see the truth, even the worst complex becomes more tolerable, for then we see the meaning and can get a little out of the entanglement. In the same sense, Fa illuminates all human beings. He never hides anything. He stretches out his hand openly to everybody. A

113

wise old medicine man gave most of the information to Maupoil and he said very nicely, literally: "All sorcerers try to describe Fa with great pomp, but though I am myself a *bokono* [a sorcerer] I would never dare to define Fa. Only the miracle-working nature which has created Fa could speak about it knowingly." So at the end of his life he said, in effect: "I don't know what Fa is, but it is this principle of truth."

Fa has many titles. Like all great powers in African representations, he is not often called by his name — they circumscribe such powers by many names which are sometimes a whole sentence or phrase, such as "Hard as a stone." Other names are: "Search and look," "He who reveals what everybody has in his heart," "Master of life," "He who transmits the messages of death": perhaps one of the most beautiful is "The sun rises and the walls get red." And there the *bokono* added this explanation: "You see, when you see the truth everything becomes clear like the sunrise." And then, ultimately, and that is interesting: "The hole which calls us into eternity."

There again is the *fenestra aeternitatis,* the window into eternity which the Africans literally call Fa, the hole which calls us into eternity. He knows the number of all those who are born, he knows the number of people who die; he holds, so to speak, everything, but he is only friendly to man. This is an archetypal parallel to the mediaeval idea of the Wisdom of God, representing the benevolent and the truthful side of Jahweh.

The dark side of reality is not in this picture of Fa and we wonder if he has not a shadow, because all archetypal figures have a shadow. Then we hear that Fa has a wife, or sometimes it is a male partner, and this partner or wife is called Gba'adu. Gba'adu is a terrible voodoo. He is not something individual, but collective and terrible. Most African medicine men say they do not want to have anything to do with Gba'adu, and they do not want his fetish in the house because Gba'adu kills and can kill at any minute. If you have his fetish it is so terrible that if you use it for magic you can kill people with it, and if you use it wrongly you might at any minute be killed yourself. It is so weighty that it is better not to handle it and therefore there are very few inititates of Gba'adu. Gba'adu wants blood; he, or she, produces life and takes it away. It is the strongest voodoo of Fa, and now listen to how they define it.

Gba'adu represents *the highest possible knowledge of oneself a man can reach.* So he is the deepest insight into the Self (we would say), which is a terrible secret and so dangerous that one cannot

114

go near it. Only Gba'adu has the secret of death and only in death can one touch this highest possible realization of oneself. Gba'adu is the secret behind Fa. Fa is the god of truth, who can accompany an individual in this life on earth, but in the moment of death one comes a step nearer to the highest self-knowledge, which is represented by Gba'adu.

Now what is the fetish of Gba'adu? The few medicine men who possess it in the secret chamber of their house, and only approach it with great precautions, say it consists of two calabash, two bowls lying upon each other. That is an image of the creation myth of those tribes who believe that in the beginning of the world god-father and god-mother lay upon each other like two calabash and procreated a lot of children and then had no space. So there is this widespread myth of the separation of the original parents, who had to be pulled apart from their eternal cohabitation so that between the gods, men and the world could be created. This kind of creative nucleus of the beginning of the world is represented by the two calabash and that is the secret of Gba'adu.

When I discovered this I was completely baffled because there suddenly appears the idea of a cosmic *conjunctio* in the problem of synchronicity, which I had not expected. But now think back over the material I have already given you: the turning of the two systems, the two planchettes, and the Older Heavenly Order and the Younger Heavenly Order interpreted by the Chinese as a cosmic union, a heaven and earth of Yin and Yang. We know that the discovery of the secret of life is interpreted in a great many mythologies as the so-called post-mortal wedding, the *hieros gamos*; in the moment of death, or just after death, there is a union of two principles which have been kept apart during life and at the time of death fall into one. It is as if those two wheels were only apart during the lifetime of a human being, but at the moment of death they melt into one, and that is interpreted as a kind of death union.

There is the same motif in the Mayan oracle of the Quiché Maya, where there is an origin legend of how the Quiché Maya found their divination oracle, the so-called Tzité oracle. According to the legend, at the beginning of the world the whole universe was silent and there was only silent water with the gods hidden in it. No creation had taken place, no wind stirred, there was no sound; but then some gods of the Quiché pantheon decided to create the world so that the gods might have worshippers.

First they created the animals, but they remained dumb so they

115

got irritated with them and said they must create something which could see and speak and which must worship and bring light to them. So they made man as a wooden or clay figure but then came the great problem — should man have eyes and a mouth? They were not sure, but at that moment they decided to make the very first Tzité oracle of the world; and while the green feather snake, which is female, united sexually with Tepëu the victor, simultaneously two divine sorcerers threw a Tzité oracle and chanted: "You maize, you Tzité, you sword, you creation, you vulva, you phallus!" — addressing the maize, the Tzité, the sword, and creation — "Look away, heart of heaven, so as not to put Tepëu and Cucumaatz to shame." Then they read the oracle, which was positive, and so they gave man mouth and eyes to worship the gods and at the same moment created the light.

We have therefore to ask in what way a synchronistic event is connected with the *coniunctio*. I think it is quite correct to say that at the moment of a synchronistic event the psyche behaves as if it were matter and matter behaves as if it belonged to an individual psyche. So there is a sort of *coniunctio* of matter and psyche and at the same time an exchange of attributes which always takes place in the *hieros gamos*. So it is really true that a synchronistic event is an act of creation and a union of two principles normally not connected. The attitude in which this can be experienced is, according to the Chinese idea — you have heard Mo Dsi — an attitude of complete sincerity, and interestingly enough, for the Chinese this is identical with playfulness.

In all primitive civilizations ritual and play cannot be separated. Rituals are played as games or play is sometimes used as ritual, and vice versa or mixed up. That is a well-known fact, exemplified by all Chinese rituals, which are a game, play, and a sacred ritual at the same time. What is the common factor psychologically? We can get an answer from the Chinese themselves: they say that a ritual or a game needs complete sincerity and complete detachment from desire and wishes. For instance, if you want to play fair, then play, for only fair play is real play. The ego which wants to win must be sacrificed for it seduces you into cheating. In spite of all the passion with which you participate, you have always to have a sacrificial attitude, knowing that you may lose, and then you have to keep face and not strangle your opponent. So one has to be completely and passionately involved, and at the same time sacrifice any kind of ego desire.

This attitude is identical with what I would call a *basic religious attitude* — to be completely involved in life and at the same time ready to lose in fair play. The rituals and the games, the Chinese go on to explain, need fixed rules and certain images to govern them. We know that all games have a pattern, rather than an image, and there are rules, but most exciting games have a certain amount of chance, i.e., of freedom: they might go one way or the other, they are not just mechanical events. The Chinese always identify the idea of lawfulness in nature as not being an absolutely determined law in the sense in which we conceive of it, but only a probability with a certain amount of play in it. It is not completely rigid, and so it is with rituals and with games in which a not quite rigid element is involved. Thus the Chinese say that through a holy, earnest play we can get closer to discovering the objective order of the universe.

121

122

CATALOGUE AND ORDER FORM
September, 1980

Publisher and General Editor
Daryl Sharp

Marie-Louise von Franz
Honorary Patron

STUDIES IN JUNGIAN PSYCHOLOGY BY JUNGIAN ANALYSTS

High quality paperbacks, professionally designed and edited

LIMITED EDITIONS

1. *The Secret Raven: Conflict and Transformation in the Life of Franz Kafka.*
Daryl Sharp. ISBN 0-919123-00-7. $10.00.

   A study of *puer aeternus* psychology and the provisional life, related to the
   conflicts in Kafka's life deriving from the mother complex, the chthonic
   shadow, and the abandoned child. Special attention to the compensatory
   significance of Kafka's dreams. Illustrated with Kafka's own drawings. Detailed index. 128 pages.

2. *The Psychological Meaning of Redemption Motifs in Fairytales.*
Marie-Louise von Franz. ISBN 0-919123-01-5. $10.00.

   A discussion of archetypal themes relevant to neurosis as a form of bewitch-
   ment. Examines the psychological significance of bathing, beating, behead-
   ing, keeping silent, right timing, eating flowers, animal skins, etc. Originally
   lectures at the C.G. Jung Institute, Zurich. Detailed index. 128 pages.

3. *On Divination and Synchronicity: The Psychology of Meaningful Chance.*
Marie-Louise von Franz. ISBN 0-919123-02-3. $12.00.

   An examination of the archetypal background to time, number, and methods of divination such as the I Ching, astrology, palmistry, dice, chaotic patterns, cards, etc. Extends and amplifies Jung's work on synchronicity, con-
   trasting Western scientific attitudes with those of the Chinese and so-called
   primitives. Originally lectures at the C.G. Jung Institute, Zurich. Illustrated.
   Detailed index. 128 pages (oversize).

4. *The Owl Was a Baker's Daughter: Obesity, Anorexia Nervosa, and the Re-
pressed Feminine.* Marion Woodman. ISBN 0-919123-03-1. $12.00.

   A pioneer work in feminine psychology, focussing on the body as mirror of
   the psyche in eating disorders and weight disturbances. Examines the loss and
   rediscovery of the feminine principle, through Jung's Association Experiment,
   case studies, and dreams. Illustrated. Detailed index. 144 pages (oversize).

5. *Introduction to the Symbolism and Psychology of Alchemy.* Marie-Louise
von Franz. ISBN 0-919123-04-X. $18.00. (November, 1980)

   An interpretation of Greek, Arabic, and European alchemical texts, designed
   as an introduction to Jung's work in alchemy. Rich in psychological insights
   from the author's own analytical experience. Invaluable for amplifying images and motifs in dreams. Originally lectures at the C.G. Jung Institute, Zürich.
   Illustrated. Detailed Index. Approx 256 pages.

PLEASE USE ATTACHED FORM TO ORDER
Prices quoted are in U.S. dollars, except for Canadian orders

Please detach and fill out both sides

ORDER FORM

Prices quoted are in U.S. dollars, except for Canadian orders

	Price	Copies	Amount
1. *The Secret Raven: Conflict and Transformation in the Life of Franz Kafka*, by Daryl Sharp	$10.00	____	____
2. *The Psychological Meaning of Redemption Motifs in Fairytales*, by Marie-Louise von Franz	$10.00	____	____
3. *On Divination and Synchronicity: The Psychology of Meaningful Chance*, by Marie-Louise von Franz	$12.00	____	____
4. *The Owl Was a Baker's Daughter: Obesity, Anorexia Nervosa, and the Repressed Feminine*, by Marion Woodman	$12.00	____	____
5. *Introduction to the Symbolism and Psychology of Alchemy*, by Marie-Louise von Franz (Nov. 1980)	$18.00	____	____

Subtotal: ____

Postage/Handling (add 60¢ per book): ____ x 60¢: ____

Enclose cheque or money order to INNER CITY BOOKS for TOTAL: ____

PREPAID ORDERS ONLY (except libraries). ORDERS FROM OUTSIDE CANADA PAY IN U.S. FUNDS.
Booksellers trade discount: 30% on subtotal of $100 minimum, on prepaid orders.
Overseas airmail: Add $2.00 per book.

(See reverse for Order Form)

NAME: _____

ADDRESS: _____

_____

_____ POSTAL CODE: _____

Send this form with your cheque or money order to:

INNER CITY BOOKS,
Box 1271, Station Q,
Toronto, Canada M4T 2P4.

Please detach and fill out both sides